AMERICAN INDIAN COUNTED CROSS-STITCH

Frankye Jones

Sterling Publishing Co., Inc.   New York

Library of Congress Cataloging-in-Publication Data

Jones, Frankye.
   [American Indian counted cross-stitch]
   Native American designs in cross stitch / Frankye Jones. — 1st pbk. ed.
      p.   cm.
   Previously published as: American Indian counted cross-stitch. c1990.
   Includes index.
   ISBN 0-8069-6976-8 (T). — ISBN 0-8069-6975-X (P)
    1. Cross-stitch—Patterns.   2. Indians of North America—Art.   I. Title.
  [TT778.C76J66 1991]
  746.44′3041—dc20   90-23672
                                                 CIP

10 9 8 7 6 5 4 3 2 1

First paperback edition published in 1991 by
Sterling Publishing Company, Inc.
387 Park Avenue South, New York, N.Y. 10016
Originally published in hard cover under the title
American Indian Counted Cross-Stitch © 1989 by Frankye Jones
Distributed in Canada by Sterling Publishing
% Canadian Manda Group, P.O. Box 920, Station U
Toronto, Ontario, Canada M8Z 5P9
Distributed in Great Britain and Europe by Cassell PLC
Villiers House, 41/47 Strand, London WC2N 5JE, England
Distributed in Australia by Capricorn Ltd.
P.O. Box 665, Lane Cove, NSW 2066
Manufactured in the United States of America
All rights reserved

Sterling ISBN 0-8069-6976-8 Trade
              0-8069-6975-X Paper

Color Photography by Nancy Palubniak

ACKNOWLEDGMENTS

The first thanks go to Betsy Klier and Art Bye, Everett, Washington, for their encouragement of the early design work, and to Betsy for her suggestion for an adobe design, which resulted in the Hopi Dwelling.

My daughter Lynnette and her husband John Marks of Muskegon, Michigan, graciously allowed us to borrow their pillow stitched with the Mountains and Lakes design, for photographing for this volume; John worked the cross-stitch and Lynnette made the pillow. Thanks also to Lynnette for stitching the Killer Whale and loaning it, also, for display in the book.

Suzanne Fujinari of The City Stitcher in Seattle provided the invaluable floss conversion chart information, and my needlepoint consultant and friend Sue Lorain advised me in the writing of the needlepoint instructions. Robert Henry taught me about the three watchers atop the Haida totem poles.

Two people were my unerring barometers on color and design; my artist friend Vicky Palm and my son Brandon Jones consistently made valuable judgment calls for which I am very grateful.

And thanks to my husband, Brock Robison, who kept himself busy all those evenings, weekends, and even during camping vacations while I was busy underneath my piles of books and floss.

Frankye Jones

Contents

Color section follows page 64.

INTRODUCTION

This book began a few years ago when I got the urge to take up cross-stitch again. My Texas grandmother had taught me years ago, as on hot summer days she provided embroidery floss and hand towels or pillow cases on which to practice, and I developed a love for the feel of the floss in its tidy little packages in every color imaginable, it seemed.

Then, one day in Seattle about 30 years after those Texas summers, I decided to recreate some American Indian designs in my favorite needlework medium of counted cross-stitch; one design led to another, and this book was born.

I grew up in Oklahoma (the state's name comes from the Choctaw, meaning "red people") and learned early to appreciate the Indian art of the Plains and of the nearby Southwest. There were colorful gatherings (American Indians call them powwows) in Anadarko, Oklahoma, where literally hundreds of Indians came each summer for the festivities dressed in brightly colored beaded costumes, headdresses and feather bustles.

There were summer visits to New Mexico, where turquoise and silver jewelry, tightly woven blankets and distinctive pottery made their impressions. As an adult, I have revisited the Southwest, and am still moved by the beauty of the artists' work there.

A later move to the Pacific Northwest brought the discovery of totems and cedar and intricate design, from the art of the Pacific Northwest Indians from Washington, Alaska, and Canada.

As the designs in this book took form, I was reminded of the American Indian history behind the art. When I stitched the tipis, for instance, I marvelled at how the buffalo was tracked and caught, how the hide was readied, how the spirits were called to inspire the design to be painted on the tipi cover, and how the finished product pleased the artists. So, because the development and history of Indian art is an integral part of the art itself, this volume includes a bit of the history of the various styles of artwork and some history of the specific tribes responsible for the designs. I hope these glimpses into the past will enhance your appreciation of these designs.

The needlework designs in this book have all been adapted from authentic designs of quillwork, beadwork, pottery, weavings, and jewelry from American Indian tribes. The designs range from the bold, brightly colored, geometric designs from the Plains, Lakes, and Eastern regions, to the highly stylized designs of browns and rust tones of the Southwest tribes, to the intricate and complex animal crest designs of the Pacific Northwest Indians.

DEDICATED TO

THE MEMORY OF MY GRANDMOTHER
GEORGIA FRENCH RUSSELL,
who taught me the stitches;

RICHARD MASSA,
who taught me the writing and the love of it;

BARBARA AND KEES,

*and to the enduring spirit and talent
of the Native American Artist.*

A single knoll rises out of the plain in Oklahoma, north and west of the Wichita Range. For my people, the Kiowas, it is an old landmark, and they gave it the name Rainy Mountain. The hardest weather in the world is there. Winter brings blizzards, hot tornadic winds arise in the spring, and in the summer the prairie is an anvil's edge. The grass turns brittle and brown, and it cracks beneath your feet. There are green belts along the rivers and creeks, linear groves of hickory and pecan, willow and witch hazel. At a distance in July or August the steaming foliage seems almost to writhe in fire. Great green and yellow grasshoppers are everywhere in the tall grass, popping up like corn to sting the flesh, and tortoises crawl about on the red earth, going nowhere in the plenty of time. Loneliness is an aspect of the land. All things in the plain are isolated; there is no confusion of objects in the eye, but one hill or one tree or one man. To look upon that landscape in the early morning, with the sun at your back, is to lose the sense of proportion. Your imagination comes to life, and this, you think, is where Creation was begun.
—*N. Scott Momaday, Kiowa Indian and Pulitzer Prize winner.*

First published in *The Reporter*, 26 January 1967. Reprinted with permission from *The Way to Rainy Mountain*, copyright 1969, The University of New Mexico Press.

6

BASICS

COUNTED CROSS-STITCH INSTRUCTIONS

MATERIALS NEEDED

To stitch the designs in counted cross-stitch you will need:

1. *Aida cloth or linen,* in your preferred count. Always purchase enough fabric so that you will have 2"–8" extra fabric on the edges, depending on how you plan to use the finished design.

    (a) Aida cloth comes in counts of 8, 11, 14, 18, 22, and these numbers mean that you will be stitching 8, 11, 14, 18, or 22 cross-stitches to the inch. The models photographed in this volume were stitched on 14-count aida (except for the Cherokee alphabet, which was stitched on 18-count). The finished size of the stitched design will be larger if you use 8- or 11-count, and smaller if you use 18- or 22-count fabric. *All finished design figures and recommendations for size of fabric to buy are based on 14-count aida, so make adjustments if you plan to use another count of fabric.* Aida cloth is sold by the yard or in precut pieces.

    (b) Linen comes in thread counts of 12, 18, 19, 20, 24, 27, and 30 threads per inch, but because cross-stitches on linen are stitched over two threads, 12-count actually equals 6 stitches to the inch, and so on. Linen is sold by the yard.

2. Embroidery floss. Floss numbers are given for DMC floss and these numbers have been used for the models for these designs, but a conversion chart on p. 93 has been included for Coats & Clark and for Bates Anchor. In general, 2 strands of floss were used on light backgrounds and 3 strands on dark backgrounds, but the number of strands depends on the type of fabric and the count of the fabric as well as individual choice. So the recommended amounts of floss to purchase for the designs here may vary, depending on these conditions.

3. Blunt tapestry needle, size 24.

4. Embroidery hoop (optional). If you do use a hoop, be sure to keep it clean (wash with damp cloth), and take it off the fabric when you are not stitching.

5. Chart. The charts in this volume are printed on 10-count (10 squares per inch) graph paper, since the larger squares are easier on the eye. This will not affect the accuracy of your design when you stitch on other fabric counts.

SOME POINTERS

1. For working on aida cloth, each square on the graph equals one cross-stitch.

2. For working on linen, each square on the graph also equals one cross-stitch, but the cross-stitch is embroidered over two threads of linen.

3. Each symbol in a square on the graph indicates a color of floss.

4. Begin a thread by holding about an inch of the end of the floss on the back of the fabric, and as the first few cross-stitches are made, secure the end of the floss under these

stitches. *Tie no knots,* for they will show through the finished work.

5. End the thread by weaving through several stitches on the back of the work and then clipping the thread. Again: *Tie no knots.*

6. All the models have been stitched on 14-count fabric or needlepoint canvas; however, if you prefer a larger or smaller size design, you may certainly use a different count material. All finished design figures, which are given for each design, are based on the design's being stitched on 14-count fabric.

GETTING STARTED

1. To prevent ravelling of the fabric, baste or tape the edges of the fabric edges.

2. Cut the floss in 15″ lengths. Divide the floss into 2 or 3 strands, depending on the directions or on your choice. Thread needle, and begin.

3. Begin stitching from the *center* of the design, in the *center* of your fabric. (However, if you prefer to begin stitching at another point of the design rather than the center, you may do so *if this point has been counted, carefully and correctly, from the center mark.*)

    (a) By counting the squares, locate the center point on the chart. This point of the design should be located in the center of your fabric.

    (b) Fold the fabric in half both horizontally and vertically to locate the center of the fabric; stitch a small piece of floss at this center point to temporarily mark the spot where stitching will begin and from which counting will proceed to other parts of the design.

4. Stitch the completed cross-stitches, each of which is essentially an X.

    (a) The *bottom* stitch of the X is completed in a left-to-right direction:

Illus. 1.

and the *top* stitch of the X is completed in a right-to-left direction:

Illus. 2.

(b) For *horizontal* rows of a particular floss color, work *all bottom stitches first,* left-to-right. Then return right-to-left, stitching *all top stitches last.*

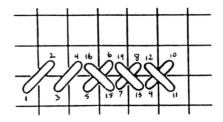

Illus. 3.

(c) For *vertical* rows of a particular floss color, complete *each* cross-stitch carefully, working *top to bottom.*

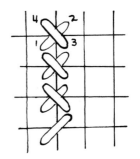

Illus. 4.

Note: It is *very* important that the stitches are always crossed in the same direction, and that horizontal and vertical rows are stitched consistently, to assure an even look to the finished work.

FINISHING

1. The finished work may be washed by hand or on the gentle machine cycle, with cold water and a gentle detergent, and it may also be dry-cleaned and pressed. If hand-pressing, iron on the back of the fabric.

2. The design may be used in a variety of ways, so feel free to use your imagination and creativity! Create items yourself, or contact your local frame shop, needlework shop, fabric shop, community center, or want ads for someone who can convert your lovely stitchery to useful items for your home.

   (a) An impressive wall display can be made by mounting and framing a collection of the designs and perhaps combining the collection with some authentic American Indian art.

   (b) The designs may be used on clothing in various ways: hatbands, headbands, belts, and borders for skirts or blouses. *Waste canvas* can be used to stitch designs onto clothing by basting the canvas onto the clothing item; after the design is finished, the canvas is pulled out, leaving the design on the fabric.

   (c) Pillow covers for the sofa, daybed, or the office can easily be made. Add coordinating borders of fabric to the design, add a back to the cover, stitch, and fill with a pillow form or other stuffing material.

   (d) Combine several of the designs in various combinations to make a wall hanging, lap throw, or quilt. Again, combine with authentic American Indian designs you may already have in the home.

NEEDLEPOINT INSTRUCTIONS

MATERIALS NEEDED

To stitch the designs in needlepoint you will need:

1. Needlepoint canvas. For best results, use mono needlepoint canvas, 14 squares to the inch. Purchase enough canvas to allow at least a 2-inch margin around the needlepoint design.

2. Needlepoint yarn. Use 3-ply Persian wool yarn. Yarn color numbers are not listed here, since models were stitched in counted cross-stitch. To find a match of yarn to the floss colors listed, find a needlework store which carries both DMC floss and needlepoint yarn, and purchase yarns which most closely match the color numbers of the floss. Experienced needlepointers will be able to estimate the amount of yarn needed, and beginning needlepointers may consult their local yarn-shop proprietor.

3. Blunt tapestry needle, size 18.

4. Chart. The charts in this volume are printed on 10-count (10 squares per inch) graph paper, since the larger squares are easier on the eye. This will not affect the accuracy of your design if you stitch on smaller or larger canvas counts.

SOME POINTERS

1. Each square on the graph equals one needlepoint stitch.

2. Each symbol in a square on the graph indicates a color of yarn.

3. Begin stitching by holding about an inch of the end of the yarn on the back of the canvas, and as the first few stitches are made, secure the end of the yarn under these stitches.

4. End the thread by weaving through several stitches on the back of the work and then clipping the thread.

5. All the models have been stitched on 14-count cross-stitch fabric (except for the Cherokee alphabet, which was stitched on 18-count), and the finished size of the design will vary from this if stitched on another size canvas.

GETTING STARTED

1. To prevent ravelling of the canvas, tape the edges of the canvas, using masking tape or paper tape.

2. Cut the yarn in 15″ to 18″ lengths.

3. Begin stitching from the *center* of the design, in the *center* of your canvas. (However, if you prefer to begin stitching at another point of the design rather than the center, you may do so *if this point has been counted, carefully and correctly, from the center mark.*)
   (a) By counting the squares, locate the center point on the chart. This point of the design should be located in the center of your canvas.
   (b) Gently fold the canvas in half both horizontally and vertically to locate the center. Stitch a small piece of yarn at this center point to temporarily mark the spot where stitching will begin and from which counting will proceed to other parts of the design.

4. Needlepoint is stitched by covering each intersection of threads on the canvas with a left-to-right, half-cross stitch.

(a) Begin by inserting the needle from the back of the canvas at the *bottom* of the intersection to be covered. Then, put the needle through the canvas to the *right* and *top* of the intersection being covered, stitching through from the front to the back. Repeat this process, always left-to-right.

(b) When the end of a row is reached and a return row must be stitched, turn the canvas upside down and work the return row stitching left-to-right, of course.

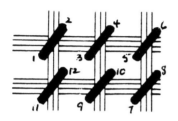

Illus. 5.

FINISHING

1. The finished work will need to be blocked, either at home or by a professional. To block at home: Roll the work in a large, wet towel for a few hours to assure the needlepoint will fully dampen. (Do not overly saturate.) Then tack the canvas on an even surface, pulling to get the entire work straight. Leave to dry. Do not press with an iron.

2. The needlepoint may, after blocking, be used to make pillows, may be framed, may be put on a chair or stool for a cushion.

Be creative!

Whether you stitch the design in counted cross-stitch or needlepoint, feel free to make creative changes of color in floss, yarn, or fabric in any of the designs in this book. Basically, any of the basic bright colors of red, blue, yellow, green, etc. are appropriate for the Plains designs and Eastern Woodlands designs, while more earth tones of browns, golds, and deep reds and blues are more appropriate for the Southwest and Pacific Northwest designs. And better yet, perhaps these designs will inspire original ones of your own!

SOUTHWEST INDIAN DESIGNS

SONG OF THE SKY LOOM

O our Mother the Earth, O our Father the Sky,
Your children are we, and with tired backs
We bring you the gifts you love.
May the warp be the white light of morning,
May the weft be the red light of evening,
May the fringes be the falling rain,
May the border be the standing rainbow.
Thus weave for us a garment of brightness,
That we may walk fittingly where birds sing.
That we may walk fittingly where grass is green.
O our Mother the Earth, O our Father the Sky.

Indians of the Four Corners, Alice Marriott, T.Y Crowell Press, Inc., reprinted with permission, Harper & Row, Publishers, Inc., New York, 1952, page 88.

SOUTHWEST INDIANS

There are many Southwest Indian artists still practising today, and, in fact, they are known internationally for their silver and turquoise jewelry and for their fine pottery and weaving.

The Hopi make distinctive overlay silver jewelry with little or no turquoise accent; the Navajo are noted for their impressive turquoise and silver jewelry pieces; and the Zuni often design with a mosaic inlay setting, using turquoise as well as other stones, often arranged into bird, animal, or human designs.

The Hopi, Zuni and Acoma are all known for their pottery, which is still made with the traditional coil method; all the pottery is hand-painted with earth tones of browns, beiges, and black and dark reds; each tribe has distinctive design styles different from one another, and each tribe has different color emphasis.

The Southwest American Indians are also quite famous for the weaving of rugs and blankets, particularly the thick and tightly woven Navajo rugs. Designs vary from area to area, and include geometrical designs, zigzags, and sandpainting figures; colors are mostly subtle, with touches of deep red.

These Indians live predominantly in Arizona and New Mexico, on both farmland and on the dry plateaus and mesas. Best known are the Navajo and the Pueblo (Hopi, Zuni, Acoma).

POTTERY DESIGN
HOPI

Illus. 6. Hopi Pottery Design. In color on p. D of color section.

FINISHED DESIGN ON 14-COUNT AIDA: Basic 4-panel strip is 1¾″ × 10″. (There is no photo of this version.)

FINISHED DESIGN ON 14-COUNT AIDA: 3 rows version is 5½″ × 7½″.

Use fiddler's cloth or a light tan linen for this design. For needlepoint, select a light beige or cream-colored yarn for the background.

Use DMC floss, 2 strands: Dark Brown, 801; Beige, 738; Rust, 920. Use 1 skein of each color for 4-panel strip, and 2 skeins of each color for the 3-row version.

This design was adapted from the pottery bowls and pots made by the Hopi. The designs of these pots are intricate and yet simple, and wonderfully pleasing to the eye. Geometric shapes are used, as are symbols of rain and water forms, and figures of birds, serpents, clouds and sky.

The pots are still made by the traditional coil method in which layers of rolled clay are smoothed together, and the pot is then shaped by hand. The designs, with graceful, flowing lines as well as precise geometric lines are then, amazingly, hand-painted onto the pot. Paints used most commonly are rust, dark red, beige and black tones.

This basic design strip of 4 panels can be used for borders on clothing and can be made as long as is needed by merely repeating the panel.

The design has been expanded here to 3 rows, which makes a beautiful pillow or framed design.

Illus. 7. Facing page: Hopi Pottery Design Chart. Numbers given here and in other charts are for DMC floss. See Conversion Chart on page 93 for Coats & Clark and Bates/Anchor numbers for all charts.

Symbol	Number	Color
o	801	Dark Brown
—	920	Rust
·	738	Beige

17

ADOBE DWELLING
HOPI

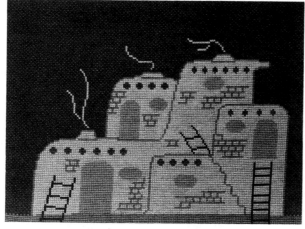

Illus. 8. Hopi Adobe Dwelling. In color on p.

FINISHED DESIGN ON 14-COUNT AIDA: 11″ × 7¾″.

Use navy blue aida cloth or linen, 11½″ × 18″, or a piece that has been sized to fit decorating needs. For needlepoint, use a navy blue yarn for the background.

Use DMC floss, 3 strands: Dark Brown, 898; Rose-beige, 3064; Rust, 434; Light Brown, 839; Dark Green, 3051; Light Blue, 793; Black, 310. Use 1 skein of all except 3064, which requires 3 skeins.

Several Southwest Tribes lived in adobe dwellings, although this particular design was inspired by a visit to a Hopi mesa. The oldest dwellings in the United States are the Southwest American Indian adobe ruins, many of which are still available for viewing by the public, mainly in Arizona and New Mexico. The Pueblo peoples built the sun-dried brick dwellings tucked into cliffs, or perched on mesas with panoramic views of the country-side; the clay dwellings provided shelter from the extreme hot sun of the area, and from the extreme cold. The structures were often 2 or 3 stories tall, with the bottom floor used only for storage, and the top floors accessible only by removable ladders.

Adobe has become the traditional architecture of the region, although the 20th-century adobe is much advanced in technique. Many suburban homes and businesses now are built of adobe.

This piece is almost alive, with the smoke from the chimneys hinting of life inside the dwelling.

Illus. 9. Below and on facing page: Adobe Dwelling Chart.

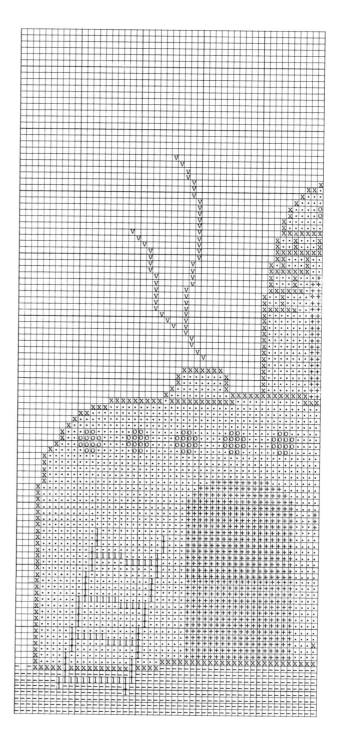

Symbol	Number	Color	Symbol	Number	Color
o	898	Brown	v	793	Blue
.	3064	Tan	1	310	Black
+	434	Brown			
x	839	Brown			
−	3051	Green*			

*This is the grass at the bottom of the dwelling. Note that the top row of grass on either side alternates: stitch, no stitch, stitch, etc.

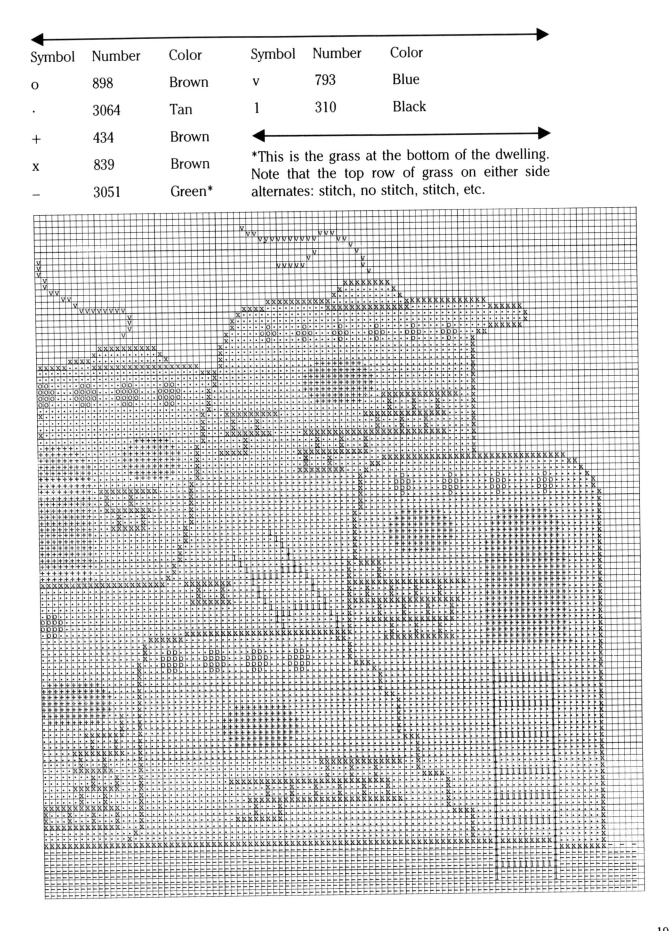

THE RAINDANCER
ZUNI

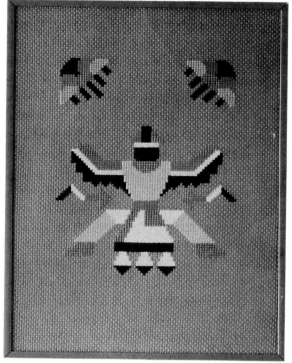

Illus. 10. Zuni Raindancer. In color on p. E of color section.

FINISHED DESIGN ON 14-COUNT AIDA: 5½″ × 6½″.

Note: Depending on the size of the finished design you wish, the rain clouds may be positioned at any distance above the raindancer. In the photo, the clouds are 10 spaces above the hat of the raindancer, while the chart shows the clouds positioned 10 spaces above the raindancer's arms.

Use rust-colored aida cloth or linen, 11″ × 11″, or any size to fit your decorating needs. For needlepoint, use a rust-colored yarn for the background.

Use DMC floss, 2 strands, or 3 strands if you prefer, of: Light Blue, 518; Blue, 517; Gold, 783; Red, 666; White, and Black. Use 1 skein of each color.

The rain clouds as depicted here are common American Indian symbols, and the raindancer is only one of the many figures of the various dances of the Indian culture. The rain dance was of major importance to the culture and ceremonies of the Southwest Indians of Arizona and New Mexico.

This design shows the Zuni characteristic of the mosaic inlay using different colors of stones and coral pieces, which is particularly evident in their world-renowned jewelry.

This design is a fun one for beginners, with many colors and small areas of each color. It may be framed or made into a pillow. Stitches up quickly.

Illus. 11. Facing page: Zuni Raindancer Chart.

Symbol	Number	Color
–	666	Red
x	310	Black
v	517	Blue
*	518	Light Blue
+	783	Gold
o		White

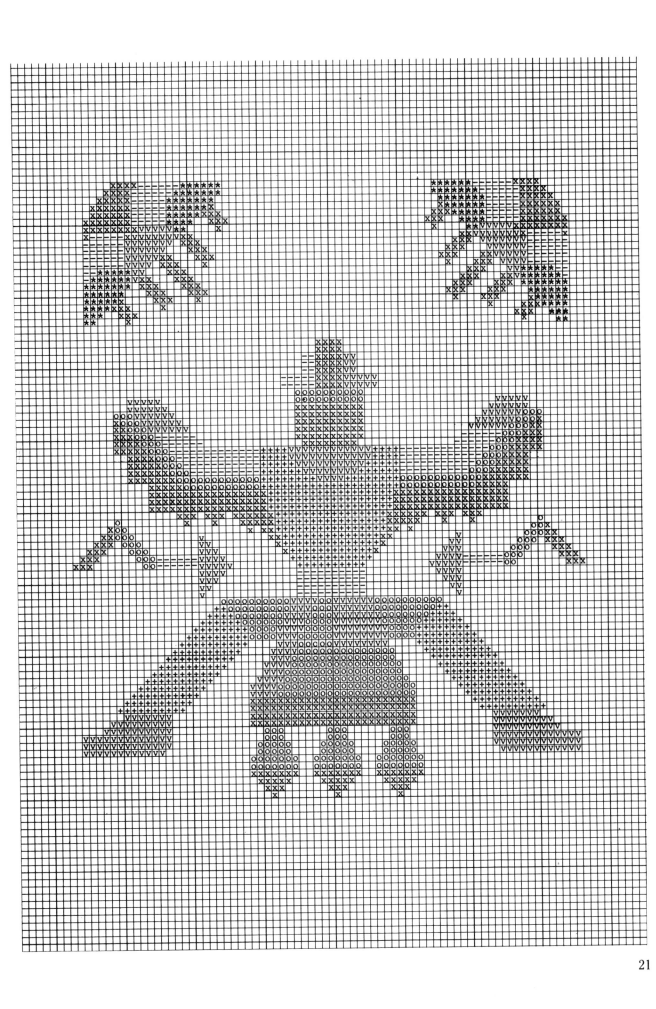

21

THUNDERBIRD
PIMA

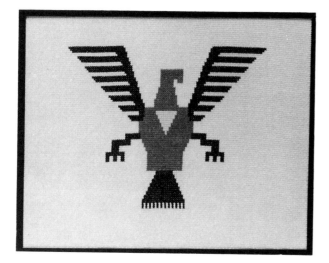

Illus. 12. Pima Thunderbird. In color on p. C of color section.

FINISHED DESIGN ON 14-COUNT AIDA: 7½″ × 6″.

Use ecru or off-white aida cloth or linen, 12″ × 12″ or larger if needed for framing or other decorative needs. For needlepoint, use an off-white or cream-colored yarn for the background.

Use DMC floss, 2 strands: Black, 310; Red, 666; Yellow, 726. One skein of each color is needed.

This is yet another representation of a thunderbird from the perspective of yet another American Indian tribe (see Apache and Pueblo thunderbird designs in this volume). The Pima, located in southern Arizona, are known for their skills in pottery and basketry, and this thunderbird was a figure used to adorn baskets, pots, and other clothing, jewelry, and ceremonial and utilitarian items. This is a very impressive piece however it is displayed and an easy piece for beginners.

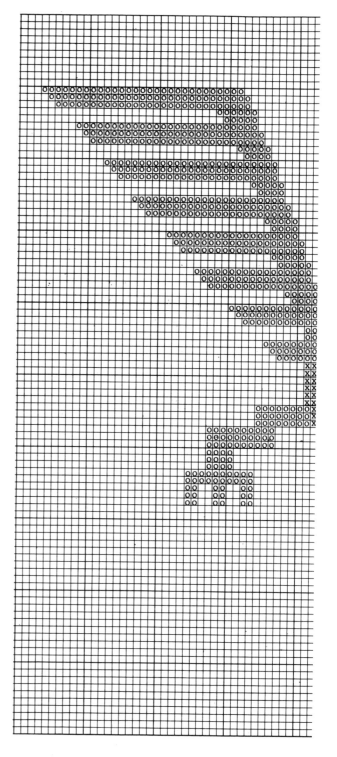

Illus. 13. Right and on facing page: Pima Thunderbird Chart.

Symbol	Number	Color
o	310	Black
x	666	Red
–	726	Yellow

THUNDERBIRD
PUEBLO

Illus. 14. Pueblo Thunderbird. In color on p. B of color section.

FINISHED DESIGN ON 14-COUNT AIDA: 4½″ × 7½″.

Use fiddler's cloth or beige or light tan linen, 11″ × 14″ or larger if more fabric is needed for decorating needs. For needlework, use a beige or light tan yarn for the background.

Use DMC floss, 2 strands: Dark Brown, 898; Chocolate Brown, 840; Black, 310; White. Uses 1 skein of each color.

This is another of the many American Indian Thunderbird designs. It was adapted from the Pueblo designs, mostly displayed on pottery in varying shades of beige and brown, with black and possibly some dark red.

This design frames well. Another idea is to make a wall hanging or small quilt with several of these Pueblo thunderbirds sewn and separated with strips or squares of complementing colors of fabric. For the creative stitcher, doing the design in other colors would be fun: I'd suggest substituting the 2 brown tones with 2 reds and/or 2 greens, 2 blues, yellow/oranges, and a mixture of the designs would make a wonderful quilt or hanging.

Illus. 15. Facing page: Pueblo Thunderbird Chart.

Symbol	Number	Color
v	898	Dark Brown
.	840	Chocolate Brown
x	310	Black
o		White

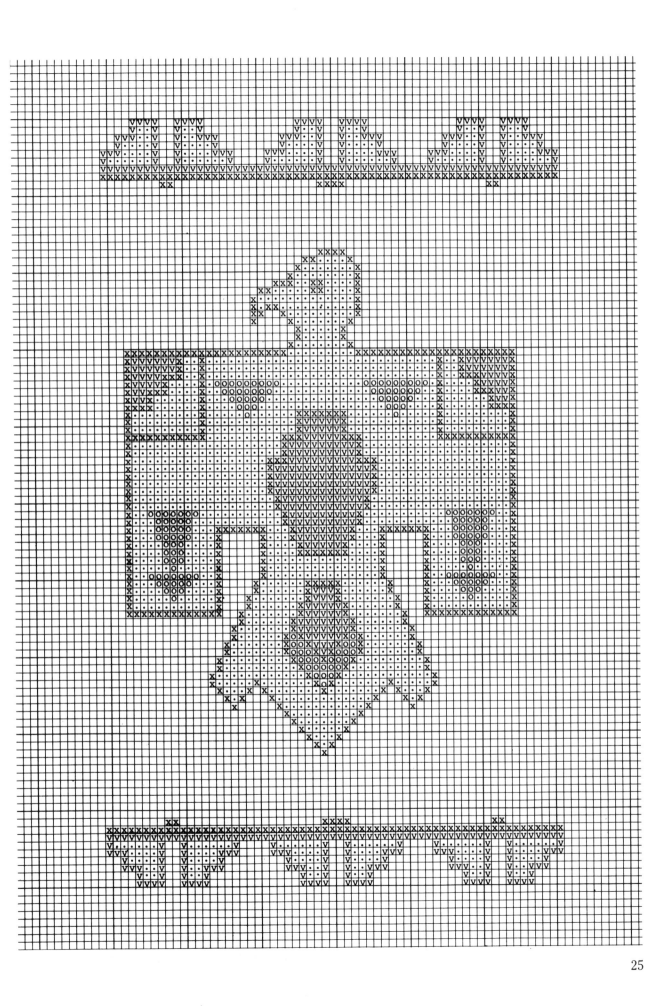

RUG DESIGN I
NAVAJO

Illus. 16. Navajo Rug Design I. In color on p. D of color section.

FINISHED DESIGN ON 14-COUNT AIDA: 5″ × 6½″.

Use fiddler's cloth for this design because it will enhance the design and emphasize its Navajo Indian rug derivation. If you prefer linen, use an unbleached shade of ivory. For needlepoint, use a light tan yarn for the background.

Use DMC floss, 2 strands: Dark Red, 304; Dark Brown, 3371; Light Brown, 840, Grey, 317. Use 1 skein of each color.

This design was adapted from the intricately designed Navajo rugs of the southwestern United States. These rugs are recognized internationally as works of great art and beauty, and the artisans who create them are highly regarded for their talent. Many of the artisans not only do the weaving, but also raise the sheep and process and spin and dye the wool before weaving; only occasionally are store-bought yarns used, since the artisans feel that their home-processed wools are superior in quality. The designs are woven from memory rather than from written-down instructions.

This piece was designed with the same color tones as Rug Design II, so that 2 similar pillows or 2 similar framed designs can be made. The design was adapted, with permission from *American Indian Beadwork*, in Ben Hunt and J.F. "Buck" Burshears, Macmillan Publishing Co., New York, 1951.

Illus. 17. Facing page: Navajo Rug Design I Chart.

Symbol	Number	Color
o	304	Dark Red
+	3371	Dark Brown
−	840	Light Brown
z	317	Grey

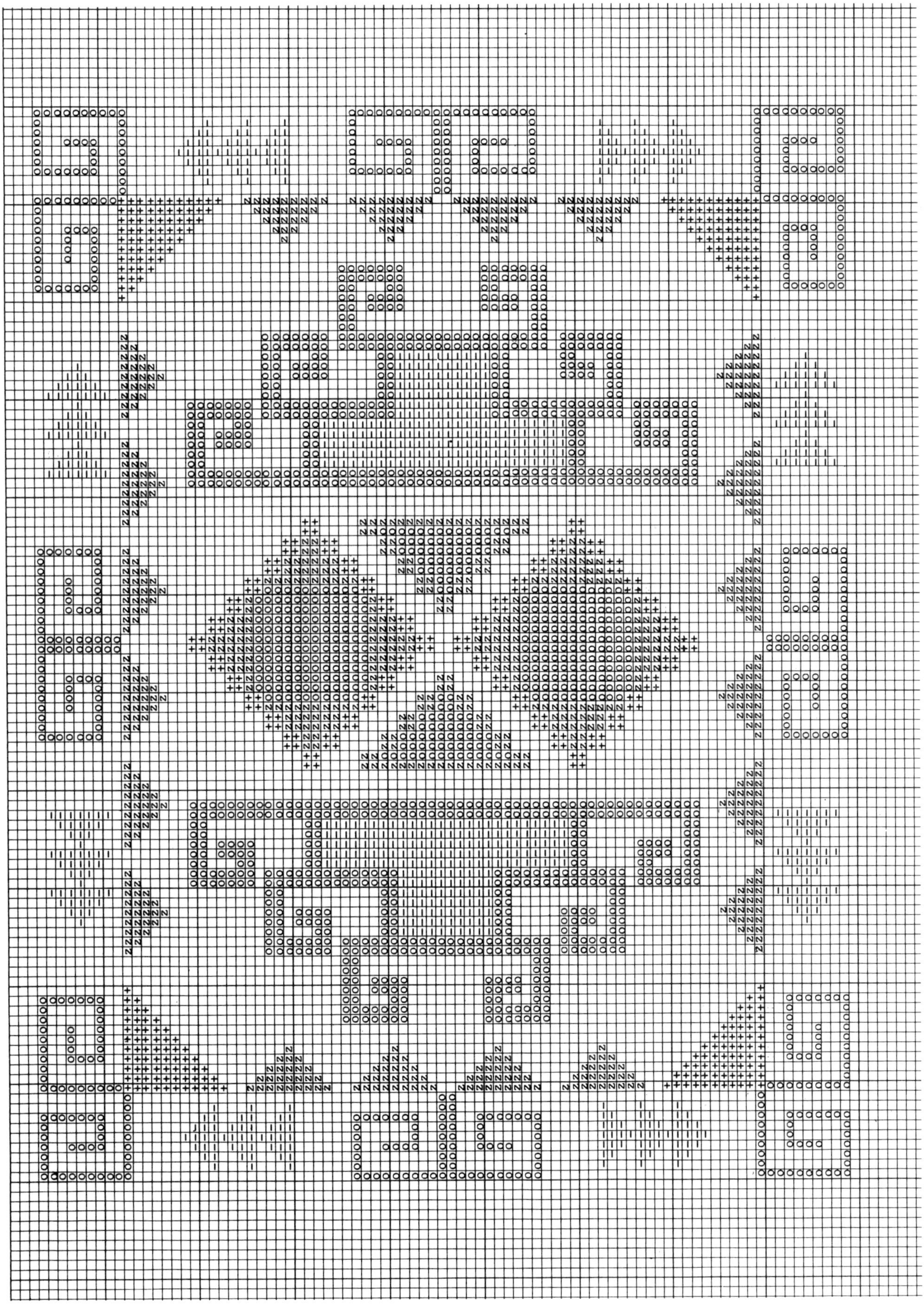

RUG DESIGN II
NAVAJO

Illus. 18. Navajo Rug Design II. In color p. H of color section.

FINISHED DESIGN ON 14-COUNT AIDA: 6¾″ × 7″.

Use fiddler's cloth for this design, because it will enhance it and emphasize the Navajo Indian rug derivation. If you prefer linen, use an un-bleached shade of ivory. For needlepoint, use a light tan yarn for the background.

Use DMC floss, 2 strands: Dark Red, 304; Dark Brown, 3371; Light Brown, 840, Grey, 317. Use 1 skein of each color.

This design, like Rug Design I, was adapted from the Navajo rug designs found in the southwestern United States. These Navajo rug designs are now recognized internationally for their beauty and skill of design. (See Rug Design I for more details.) This pattern was designed to be able to match easily with Rug Design I for decorating in the home.

Illus. 19. Facing page: Navajo Rug Design II Chart.

Symbol	Number	Color
s	304	Dark Red
+	317	Grey
−	840	Light Brown
z	3371	Dark Brown

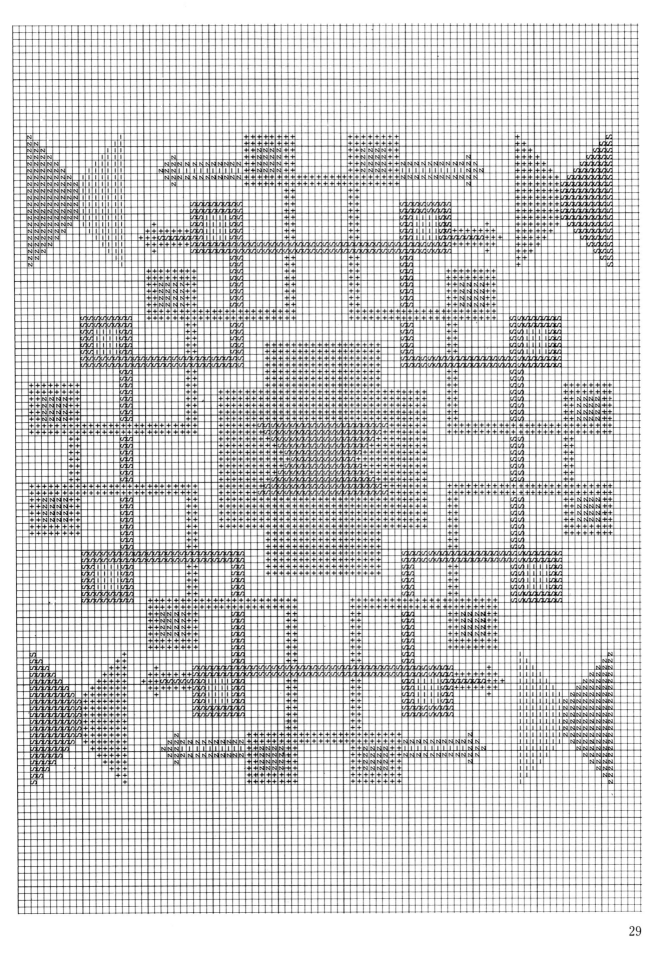

FEMALE YEI FIGURES
NAVAJO

FINISHED DESIGN ON 14-COUNT AIDA: 6″ × 8½″.

Use rust-colored aida cloth or linen, 10″ × 12″, or size to accommodate decorating needs. For needlepoint, use a rust-colored yarn for the background.

Use DMC floss, 2 strands (you may use 3 strands if you prefer, since the background is dark): Brown, 898; Black, 310; Red, 666; Grey, 414; White; Dark Brown, 3371; Turquoise, 807; Rose, 3688; and Pink, 3689. One skein of each is needed, although you may need 2 skeins of 3688 and 3689 if 3 strands are used.

This design was adapted from sandpainting designs displayed on wall hangings and rugs by the Navajo for purchase by the general public. The figures depicted here are female Yeibichai figures: Navajo supernatural beings, which are represented by masked dancers. The square face masks worn by the dancers or figures indicate that they are female (see the Male Yei Figures also in this volume, noted by their round face masks).

Original sandpainting designs were made of crushed red sandstone, charcoal and sand, for religious and curative purposes; the sand pictures were actually made on the ground in a pre-determined design for a specific ceremony. Contemporary sandpainting designs which are sold to the public on wall hangings and rugs and are not used for religious or curative Navajo ceremonies, are purposely designed with discrepancies from the original design; this shows reverence for the spiritual powers of the original designs.

THE RAINBOW GUARDIAN: The figures of a sandpainting are all said to "enter" from the top (or East) of the painting, which leaves the sides and bottom unprotected; thus, the rainbow guardian figure embraces those unprotected three sides of the painting and provides the needed protection to the rest of the figures.

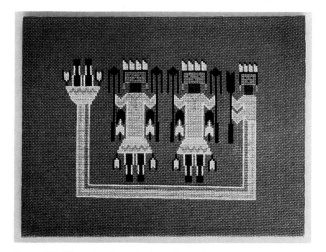

Illus. 20. Navajo Female Yei Figures. In color on p. B of color section.

Illus. 21. Facing page: Navajo Female Yei Figures Chart.

Symbol	Number	Color
x		White
–	3688	Rose
*	3689	Pink
.	414	Grey
v	807	Turquoise
o	310	Black
+	3371	Dark Brown
e	898	Brown
r	666	Red

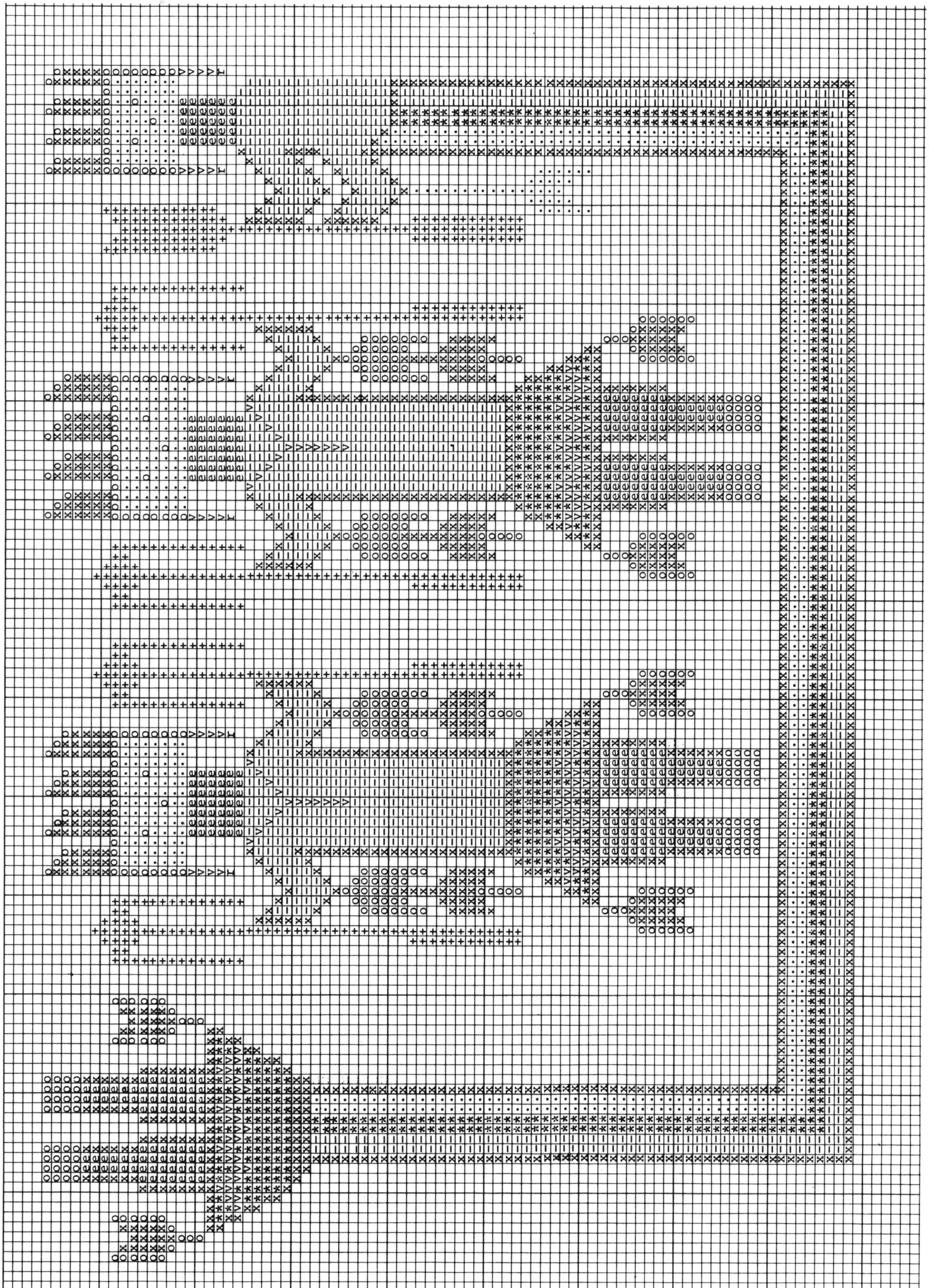

MALE YEI FIGURES
NAVAJO

Illus. 22. Navajo Male Yei Figures. In color p. D of color section.

FINISHED DESIGN ON 14-COUNT AIDA: 8″ × 6″.

Use ecru or off-white aida cloth or linen. For needlepoint, use an ivory or off-white yarn for the background.

Use 2 strands of DMC floss: Black, 310; Turquoise, 958; Brown, 356; Purple, 553; Dark Rose, 3687; Light Rose, 3688; Dark Blue, 312; Yellow, 444; Dark Red, 815. One skein of each color is needed.

The Male Yei Figures are a companion piece to the Female Yei Figures. Note the round masks of the male Yei dancers, as opposed to the square masks of the female Yei dancers. (See the description of the Female Yei Figures for an explanation of the rainbow figure which borders this design.)

Because the original sandpaintings were made with crushed stones and sands from the earth, the colors of the sandpaintings were soft browns, rose tones, with black from charcoal, with some red and yellow and white sands, and plant pollens. The sandpaintings were made for special curing or religious purposes and were always destroyed by sundown of the same day they were created and used.

Illus. 23. Facing page: Navajo Male Yei Figures Chart.

Symbol	Number	Color
*	310	Black
o	958	Turquoise
c	356	Tan/Reddish Brown
v	553	Purple
–	3687	Dark Rose
r	312	Dark Blue
x	3688	Light Rose
·	444	Yellow
+	815	Dark Red

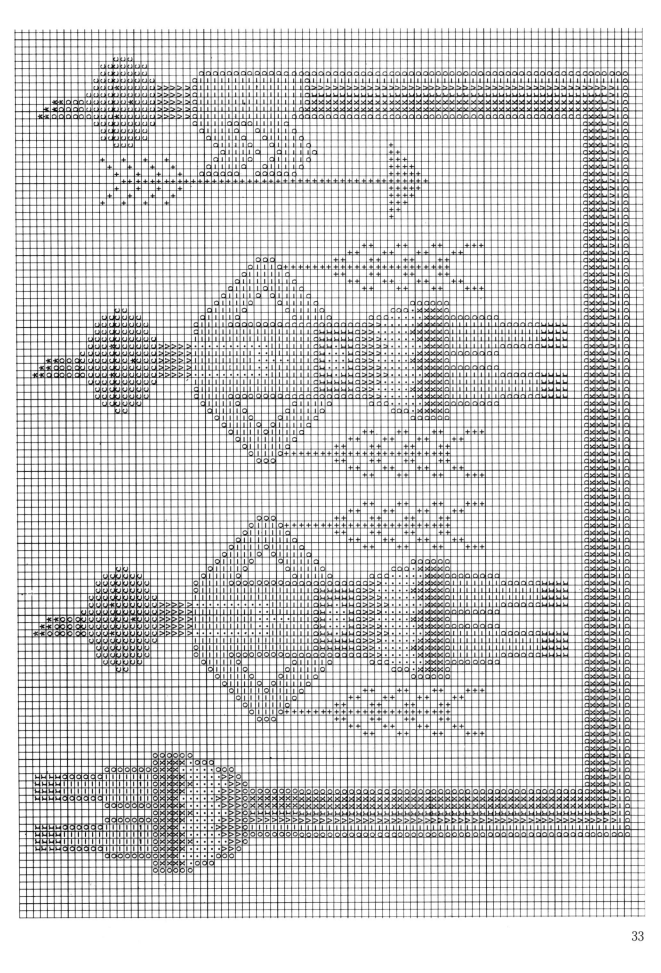

MOTHER EARTH, FATHER SKY NAVAJO

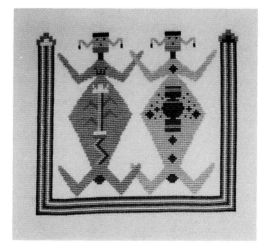

Illus. 24. Navajo Mother Earth, Father Sky. In color p. G of color section.

FINISHED DESIGN ON 14-COUNT AIDA: 8″ × 7″.

Use ecru or off-white Aida cloth or linen. For needlepoint, use an off-white yarn for the background.

Use 2 strands of DMC floss: Orange/Rust, 900; Yellow, 445; Light Blue, 809; Dark Blue, 820; Purple, 550; Turquoise, 958; Green, 989; Light Brown, 729; Dark Brown, 801; Light Rose, 316; Black, 310. Use 1 skein each, though you may possibly need 2 skeins of 809 and 989.

These two figures, Mother Earth and Father Sky, are only two of the many figures used in ceremonial life: in sandpaintings, in dance, and in stories and myth. These and other figures were important deities, a way for the people to show their high regard for the powers of the earth and sky because it was the fertile soil, rain and sun that made possible the crops for food to sustain their families and their lives. Note that these figures, like the Yeibeichai figures, are also wearing masks, for no one is allowed to see the faces of such important deities as Mother Earth and Father Sky.

Inside the "belly" of the Mother Earth Figure is portrayed the corn plant, the food staple of the Southwest Indian people, and of course inside the

figure of Father Sky are symbols for the sun, moon and stars. (See the description of the Female Yei Figures for an explanation of the rainbow border in this design.)

Illus. 25. Facing page: Navajo Mother Earth, Father Sky Chart.

Symbol	Number	Color
–	809	Light Blue
v	820	Dark Blue
c	958	Turquoise
x	550	Purple
.	989	Green
+	801	Dark Brown
r	729	Light Brown
o	900	Orange/Rust
s	445	Yellow
*	310	Black
l	316	Light Rose

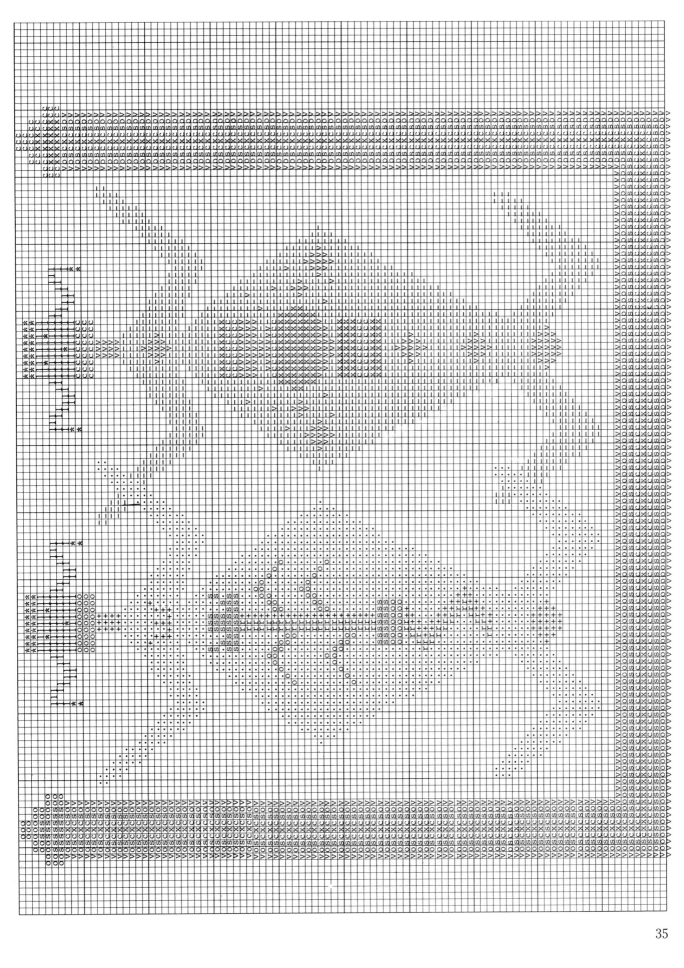

THUNDERBIRD DESIGN
APACHE

Illus. 26. Apache Thunderbird Design. In color on p. H of color section.

FINISHED DESIGN ON 14-COUNT AIDA: 6″ × 7¾″.

Use rust-colored aida cloth or linen. For needlepoint, use rust-colored yarn for the background.

Use 3 strands of DMC floss: Dark Blue, 796; Red, 666; Dark Turquoise, 958; Light Turquoise, 959; Yellow, 444; Black, 310. Use 2 skeins of white and 958, and 1 skein of all other colors.

This design is adapted from shield designs used by the Apache, who were powerful protectors of their property and families. Shields were used both for protection in battle and for use in ceremonial life. The shields were made from the heaviest buffalo hides and were used by the American Indians of the Plains as well as of the Southwest, though the shield designs varied from area to area and tribe to tribe. Some shields, for instance, were decorated with feathers, others were not. Designs on the shields were important, for the design was believed to be a powerful deterrent to the enemy; in some tribes, a cover was kept over the shield until just before it was used in battle, so that the strength of the design would not be weakened before it was actually needed to help defeat the enemy.

Illus. 27. Facing page: Apache Thunderbird Chart.

Symbol	Number	Color
x	796	Dark Blue
o	666	Red
–	444	Yellow
1	958	Dark Turquoise
*	959	Light Turquoise
.		White
c	310	Black

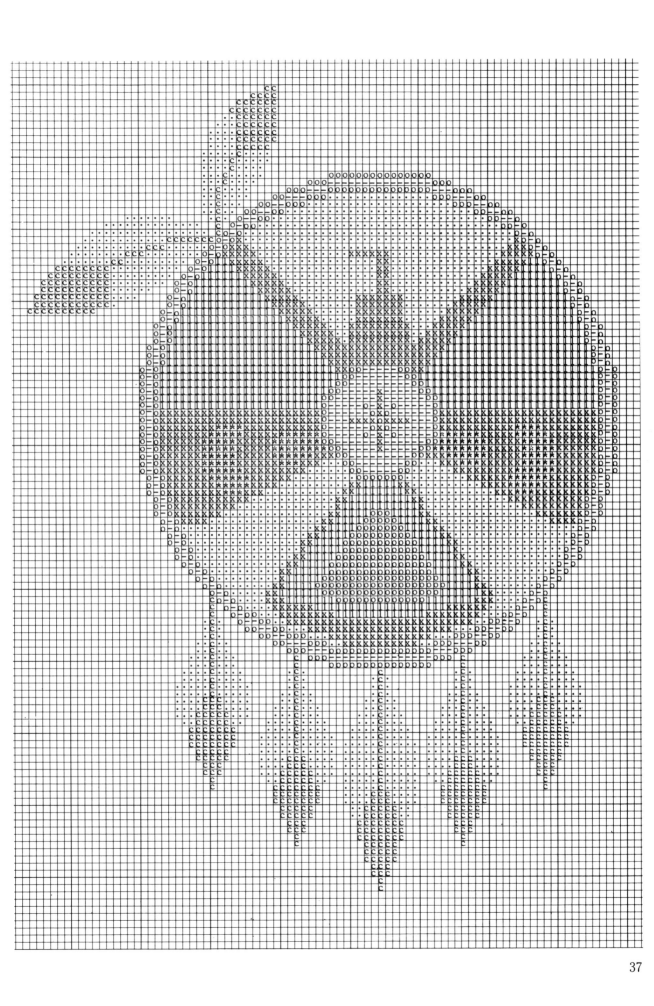

37

PLAINS INDIAN
DESIGNS

*First Snowfall of the Season—the bottom layer of white—
    a few more feet to come, yet—to make the Outdoors bright.
By middle of the Winter—You'll stand above the door—
    climb down to get inside, then—lay your shovel on the floor.
Inside you'll feel quite sheltered—as though beneath the ground.
    Hang your food-pots over the fire—as it's spreading its warmth around.
While snowflakes strike the tipi—and wind flies through the Air—
    You'll feel as One with Nature—for Nature's with you in there.
—Adolf Hungry Wolf*

Tipi Life, Adolf Hungry Wolf, Good Medicine Books, Alberta, 1972. Reprinted with permission.

PLAINS INDIANS

The arts of the American Indians who lived on the Plains varied in detail from tribe to tribe, as did their ceremonies and customs, although generally, their art is recognized by its geometric designs and bright colors. The Plains Indians are known specifically for their work of sewing porcupine quills (first flattened and dyed) onto hides; in fact, this art is unique and is found nowhere else in the world. The quill-work did, of course, eventually give way to bead-work when glass beads were brought to North America. The quill and bead designs were used on clothing, moccasins, headbands, and other accessories, and many of these pieces were stunning pieces of work.

The Plains tribes are also known for their colorful painted tipis; they came to use the tipi cover as artist's canvas for expressions of religious, ceremonial, and tribal customs and beliefs. These tipis, each of which were made of several buffalo hides, resisted the strong winds of the Plains, and were easily moved from location to location in the nomadic life required by the movement of the buffalo. The buffalo provided food, clothing, and tools, as well as the tipi cover. The Blackfoot Indians are especially well-known for their painted tipis; usual designs were horizontal borders, circular designs, scenes of battle, and of course various depictions of the buffalo.

The Indians of the Plains lived on the mostly flat area between the Rockies on the west and the Mississippi on the east, from Mexico to Canada. There were many Plains tribes located in different parts of the Plains area, and some of the better known were: Southern Plains—Kiowa, Comanche; Central Plains—Western Sioux, Crow, Cheyenne, and Arapaho; and in the Southeast Plains—Pawnee and Ponca.

THREE TIPIS
BLACKFOOT

Illus. 28. Blackfoot Three Tipis. In color on p. F of color section.

FINISHED DESIGN ON 14-COUNT AIDA: 5½″ × 9″.

Use maize (light yellow) aida cloth or linen. (Beige or off-white will do, if you prefer, or if maize is unavailable.) Use fabric 11″ × 14″. For needlepoint, use a pale yellow yarn for the background.

Use 1 skein of each color, DMC floss, 2 strands as follows:

MIDDLE TIPI COLORS—Main tipi color, Rust, 420; tipi trim, Deep Red, 815; stars on trim, Off-white, 712; sun design, Yellow, 725; tipi door and lining, Light Beige, 422; tipi fasteners, Black, 310; tipi poles, Brown, 300.

RIGHT TIPI COLORS—Main tipi color, Orange, 721; tipi trim, Purple, 553; tipi trim, Green, 702; tipi fasteners, Black, 310; tipi poles, Dark Brown, 898; tipi poles, Light Brown, 434.

LEFT TIPI COLORS—Main tipi color, Light Blue, 793; tipi trim and outline, Dark Blue, 312; tipi circle trims, Light Beige, 422; buffalo design, Dark Brown, 898; buffalo horns and eye, Off-white, 712; buffalo nose, Black, 310; tipi poles, 975 and 920.

One of the most unusual artistic achievements of the American Indian is the painted tipi of the Plains tribes. The word "tipi" comes from the Dakota Indian language, meaning "dwelling," or "they dwell." Designs for the tipi covers often had religious and ceremonial meaning and were said to be sometimes inspired by visions seen by the artist. These painted tipis were reserved for group use and for use by tribal leaders and other important tribe members (such as tipi artists). Individual tipis for most families were left undecorated. Some of the common designs for the painted tipis were circles or rosettes (see

Arapaho Rosette design), horizontal borders, depictions of animals, and battle scenes.

This is a wonderfully colorful piece to stitch and enjoy.

Illus. 29. Color Code. Pages 44 and 45: Blackfoot Three Tipis Chart.

◄─────────────────────────►

Left Tipi

Symbol	Number	Color
x	312	Dark Blue
*	793	Light Blue
+	422	Light Beige
c	898	Brown
▼	712	Off-white
●	310	Black
U	975	Brown
T	920	Rust

Middle Tipi

Symbol	Number	Color
1	420	Rust
S	815	Deep Red
■	712	Off-white
r	725	Yellow
A	422	Light Beige
8	310	Black
o	300	Brown

Right Tipi

Symbol	Number	Color
–	721	Orange
*	553	Purple
V	702	Green
8	310	Black
W	898	Dark Brown
E	434	Light Brown

◄─────────────────────────►

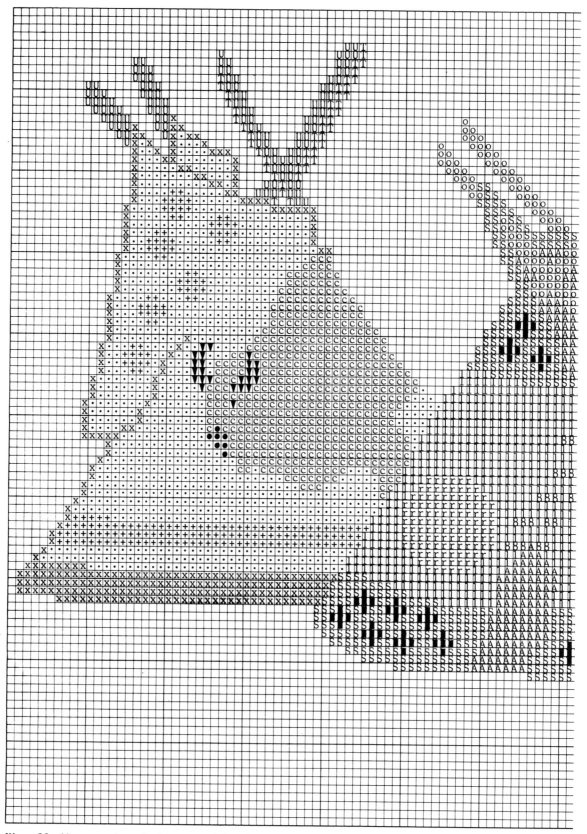

Illus. 29. Above and on facing page: Blackfoot Three
Tipis Chart.

TIPI WITH BUFFALO, SIDE VIEW BLACKFOOT

Illus. 30. Blackfoot Tipi with Buffalo, Side View. (Not shown in color).

FINISHED DESIGN ON 14-COUNT AIDA: 7¾″ × 7¾″.

Use fiddler's cloth or an off-white linen. For needlepoint, use an off-white or light tan yarn for the background.

Use 2 strands of DMC floss: Dark Blue, 311; Blue, 809; Dark Red, 815; Buffalo: Brown, 801; nose and hoof: Black, 310; horns and eye: 950; tipi poles: Browns, 938, 780. Use 2 skeins of 809, 1 skein of other colors.

One of the more common depictions on the tipi covers was, of course, the buffalo, which was central to the survival of the Plains Indians, since they derived so much of their food, clothing, and other necessities (such as the tipi cover itself) from this one source. The buffalo was pictured large or small, alone or in pictures with other animals, or in hunting scenes.

Because the Plains Indians depended so much on the buffalo for their survival, they had to follow the buffalo herds wherever they went; the result was a nomadic life for the tribes, and of course the very portable tipi was a perfect home for such a life. Depending on the size of the tipi, there were many buffalo hides needed for each structure; it is said that for the very large tipis, up to 40 hides were used.

Symbol	Number	Color
x	311	Dark Blue
.	809	Light Blue
*	815	Dark Red
o	801	Brown
●	310	Black
▼	950	Beige
U	938	Dark Brown
T	780	Brown

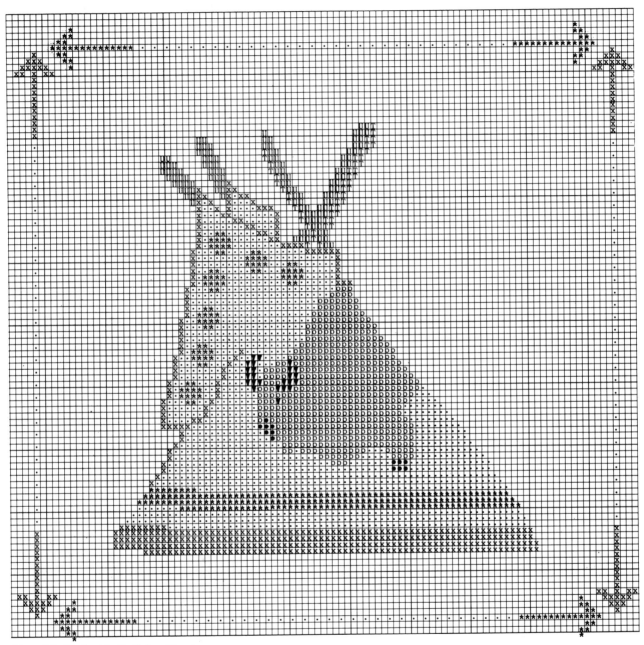

Illus. 31. Tipi with Buffalo, Chart.

TIPI, FRONT VIEW
BLACKFOOT

Illus. 32. Blackfoot Tipi, Front View. In color on p. C of color section.

FINISHED DESIGN ON 14-COUNT AIDA: 7¼″ × 7⅜″.

Use 14-count fiddler's cloth or an off-white linen. For needlepoint, use a light tan yarn for the background.

Use 2 strands of DMC floss: Green, 912; Light Rust, 922; Yellow, 743; Dark Brown, 3371; Light Green, 955; Brown and Rusts: 938, 434, 801; Orange, 740; and Green, 699. Use 1 skein of each color.

This view of the tipi shows the front opening which was the entry-way, and the fasteners which made it possible to close the tipi to the weather outside. The opening in the top drew out the smoke from the cook and warming fires. For more details on the tipis see the *Tipi with Buffalo—Side View*, and *Three Tipis*, both in this volume.

Symbol	Number	Color
–	912	Green
1	922	Brown/Rust
*	743	Yellow
C	3371	Dark Brown
·	955	Light Green
O	938	Tipi Pole
S	434	Tipi Pole
+	801	Tipi Pole
x	699	Dark Green Border
U	740	Orange Border

Illus. 33. Blackfoot Tipi, Front View, Chart.

CIRCLE DESIGN
ARAPAHO

Illus. 34. Arapaho Circle Design. In color on p. A of color section.

FINISHED DESIGN ON 14-COUNT AIDA: 4¼″ edge to edge of circle.

Use ecru or off-white aida cloth or linen, 11″ × 11″ or larger if more fabric is needed for framing or other decorative needs. For needlepoint, use an off-white or ivory yarn for the background.

Use DMC floss, 2 strands: Gold, 783; Black, 310; White; Rose, 326. One skein of each color is needed.

This design was adapted from a beaded tipi decoration which was used as as adornment on the painted tipis; circle designs varied and were a common adornment on tipis of many Plains tribes. Like other Plains tribes, the Arapaho are known for their striking geometric designs of quill and beadwork, and although they are also known for their bright color tones, designs such as this one, with more subtle hues and unusual color combinations, were also common.

This is a lovely design for circular pillows, but it is also simple and striking in a frame, and it may be combined with other American Indian circular designs in hangings or pillow sets, etc.

Illus. 35. Facing page: Arapaho Circle Chart.

Symbol	Number	Color
o	310	Black
s		White
–	326	Rose
·	783	Gold

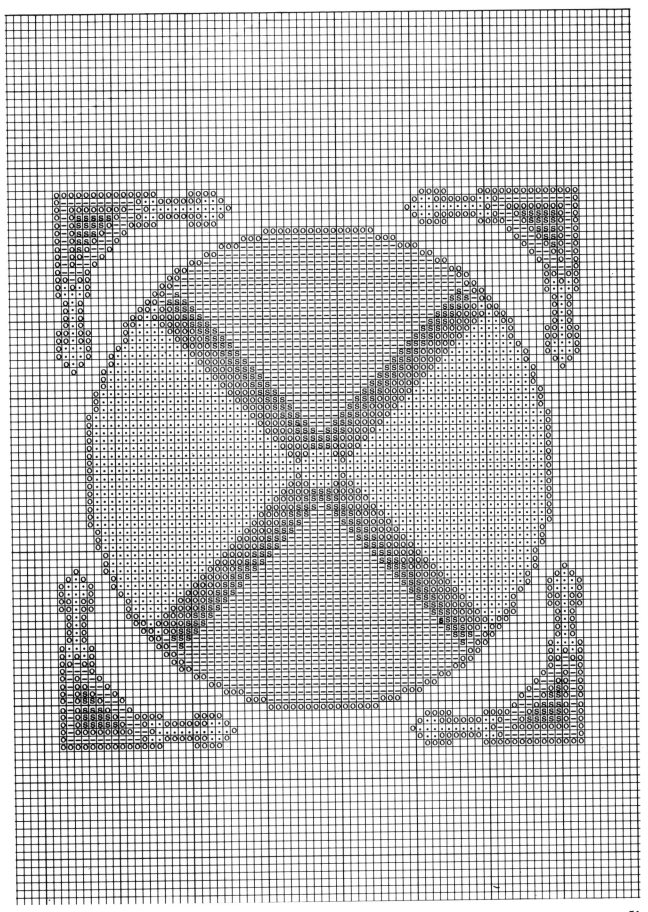

MOUNTAINS AND LAKES
SIOUX

Illus. 36. Sioux Mountains and Lakes. In color on p. E of color section.

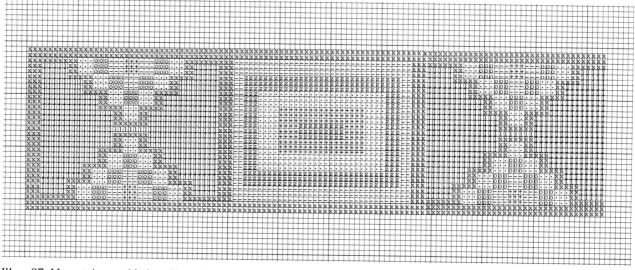

Illus. 37. Mountains and Lakes Chart for one row. Above and on facing page.

FINISHED BORDER DESIGN: Can be made as long as you wish by repeating the design. The basic design shown, stitched in 14-count aida, is 8½″ × 2¼″. Use one skein of each color. (See Illus. 37.)

Note: Decide which color you want for the 3-row borders (the x's on the charts): 796 Dark Blue or 798 Bright Blue; then, depending on which color you use for the borders, you then use the other color (the one you do NOT choose for the borders) for the large sections in the mountains area (the 1's on the charts).

Mountains and Lakes—Sioux (color code applies to both designs)

x	796	Dark Blue (as in pillow photo)
		OR
	798	Bright Blue (as in figure 1 photo)
1	798	Bright Blue (as in figure 1 photo)
		OR
	796	Dark Blue (as in pillow photo)
·	444	Yellow
+	601	Pink
z	701	Green
−	552	Purple
o	740	Orange

FINISHED DESIGN, 4 ROWS ON 14-COUNT AIDA: 8¾″ × 11⅛″. This version, as the photo shows, is different from the border design version in that the background colors are different, i.e., the main background color in this version is the dark blue (796) whereas the background color in the border version is the lighter blue (798). Either background color is fine for either version. (See Illus. 38.)

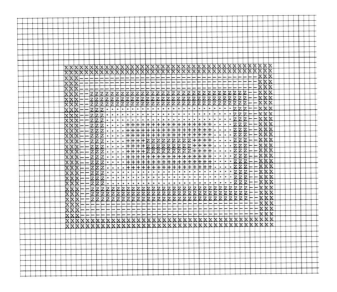

Use ecru, white or ivory aida cloth or linen. For needlepoint, use an ivory or cream-colored yarn for the background.

Use DMC floss, 2 strands: Bright Blue, 798; Yellow, 444; Orange, 740; Lavender, 552; Bright Rose, 601; Green, 701. Use 3 strands of: Dark Blue, 796. Use 2 skeins of 796 and 798 and 1 skein each of all the other colors.

This brilliantly colorful design is a Sioux design called "mountains and lakes." The portion of the design with the small, colorful, stair-step squares is the "mountains" and the rectangles of bright color with green in the center are the "lakes." This is a good example of the Sioux designs, which involved the use of geometric triangles, crosses, and rectangles in the work.

This particular design was adapted from a beaded design, which would have been used on clothing, and is a wonderful example of the Plains Indian use of bright colors. The basic strip of three panels can be extended by repeating the panels and can be used as borders on clothing or other items. The version of four rows can be used for a pillow, as pictured, or can be beautifully framed.

This design was adapted with permission from *American Indian Beadwork*, W. Ben Hunt and J.F. "Buck" Burshears, Macmillan Publishing Co., New York, 1951.

Illus. 38. Mountains and Lakes extended to four rows.
In color on cover. Chart on following pages.

Illus. 39. Above and on facing page: Mountains and
Lakes Chart.

54

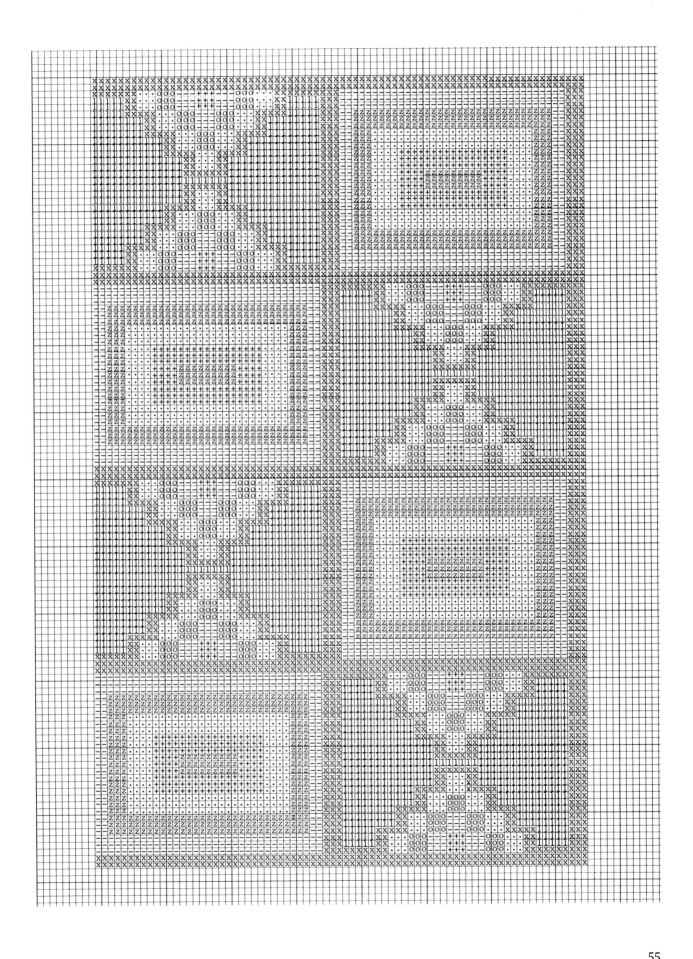

SADDLEBAG DESIGN I CROW

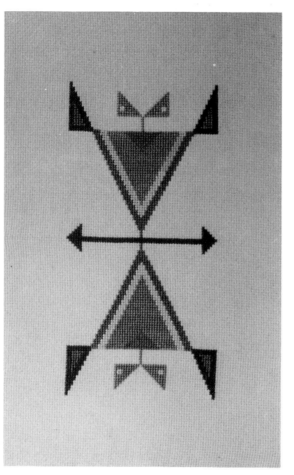

Illus. 40. Crow Geometric Saddlebag Design I. In color on p. B of color section.

FINISHED DESIGN ON 14-COUNT AIDA: 4½″ × 9″.

Use light blue aida cloth or linen. For needlepoint, use a light blue yarn for the background.

Use DMC floss, 3 strands: Blue, 798; Yellow, 726; Red, 321; Green, 989. Use 1 skein of each color.

This piece is an excellent example of the large, elongated triangular forms which exemplifies the Crow art. This sort of design was used on saddlebags and pipebags and was usually sewn onto hides with quills and later, of course, with beads.

Illus. 41. Facing page: Crow Geometric Saddlebag Design I Chart.

Symbol	Number	Color
o	321	Red
x	798	Blue
.	726	Yellow
−	989	Green

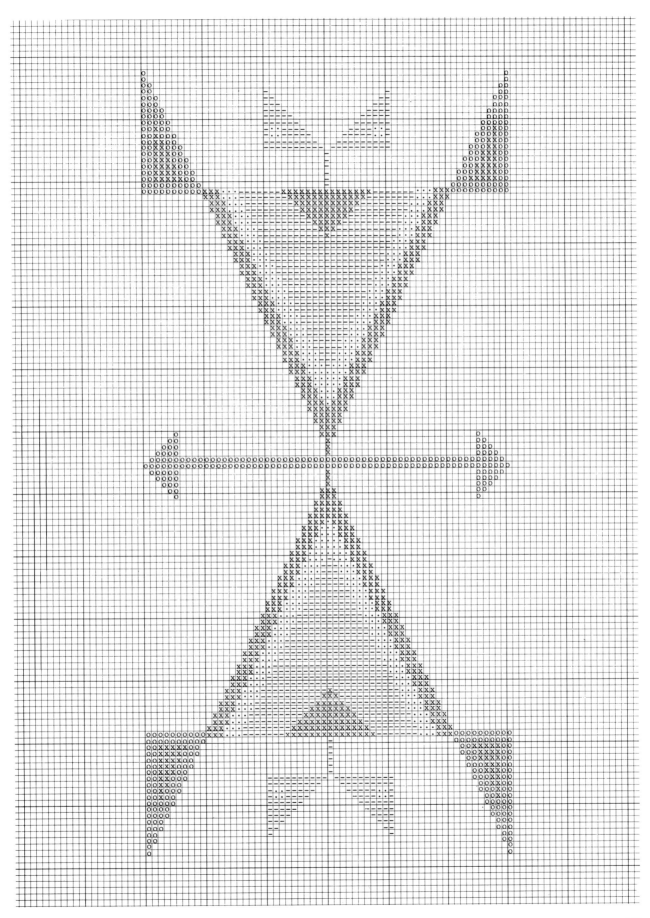

SADDLEBAG DESIGN II
PLAINS

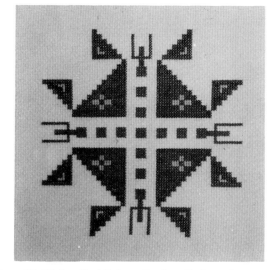

Illus. 42. Plains Saddlebag Design II. In color on p. F of color section.

FINISHED DESIGN ON 14-COUNT AIDA: Approximately 6″ × 6″ square.

This design can be sewn onto several choices of background aida fabric or linen (white, ivory, fiddler's cloth, maize, light blue). The version in the photo was sewn on ecru aida. For needlepoint, use white, ivory, beige, pale yellow, or light blue yarn for the background.

Use DMC floss, 2 strands: Red, 666; Blue, 796; Yellow, 444. Use 1 skein of each color.

This is a typical design, used by Plains tribes on saddlebags and pipebags, and again is an example of the geometric style, and, in particular, an example of the Plains artist's juxtaposing of triangles as the basis of a design. Early American Indians sewed the designs with porcupine quills which they first cut and dyed; this porcupine quill art preceded the use of glass beads and is unique. Designs such as this one (as well as the Ojibway headband and Crow pipebag designs) were usually sewn with the quills or beads onto hides.

This design was adapted with permission from *American Indian Beadwork*, W. Ben Hunt and J.F. "Buck" Burshears, Macmillan Publishing Co., New York, 1951.

Symbol	Number	Color
o	666	Red
.	444	Yellow
—	796	Blue

Illus. 43. Plains Saddlebag Design II Chart.

GEOMETRIC DESIGN I
PLAINS

Illus. 44. Plains Geometric Design I. In color on p. E of color section.

FINISHED DESIGN ON 14-COUNT AIDA: 6″ × 6½″.

Use ecru or off-white aida cloth or linen. For needlepoint, use an ivory or off-white yarn for the background.

Use DMC floss, 2 strands: Dark Blue, 336; Green, 702; Gold, 783; Purple, 552; Light Blue, 322; Light Turquoise, 993; Red, 304; Orange 740. Use 1 skein of each color.

This design was adapted from a very old corn-husk bag and the tribe is uncertain, though it is definitely from the Plains area. These bags were woven by tribes in the Lakes and Prairie areas as well as the Plains areas, and were used for carrying items, and were carried on horseback when travelling long distances. This piece is a marvelous combination of 8 different colors and is a fine example of the geometric style with triangles and rectangles.

This design is very nice simply framed and hung in a setting of other Native American items or sewn into a pillow for a striking accent.

Illus. 45. Facing Page: Plains Geometric Design I Chart.

Symbol	Number	Color
l	336	Dark Blue
s	702	Green
o	740	Orange
x	304	Red
v	322	Light Blue
c	993	Turquoise
.	552	Purple
—	783	Gold

GEOMETRIC DESIGN II
PLAINS

Illus. 46. Plains Geometric Design II. In color on p. C
of color section.

FINISHED DESIGN ON 14-COUNT AIDA: 5⅝″ ×
7¼″.

Use red aida cloth or linen. For needlepoint,
use a red yarn for the background.

Use 3 strands of DMC floss: Yellow, 973; Blue,
793; White; Green, 912; and Orange, 740. Use 1
skein of each color.

This piece was adapted from a beaded moc-
casin design, and with the red background, the
counted cross-stitch version looks beaded, too.
Again, the familiar triangles are spread out in varying combinations and positions, and are of course
done in very bright colors. This would have been
beaded onto a saddlebag or pipebag, or knee-high
moccasins.

Illus. 47. Facing page: Plains Geometric Design II Chart.

Symbol	Number	Color
o	973	Yellow
.	793	Blue
–	912	Green
1	740	Orange
x		White

Top: Pacific Northwest Bear Design. See p. 72.

.Center: Arapaho Circle Design. See p. 50.

Bottom: Ojibway Headband. See p. 82. (Instructions also given for 3-row version of design.)

Top: Navajo Female Yei Figures. See p. 30.

Lower right: Crow Geometric Saddlebag Design I. See p. 56.

Bottom: Pueblo Thunderbird Design. See p. 24.

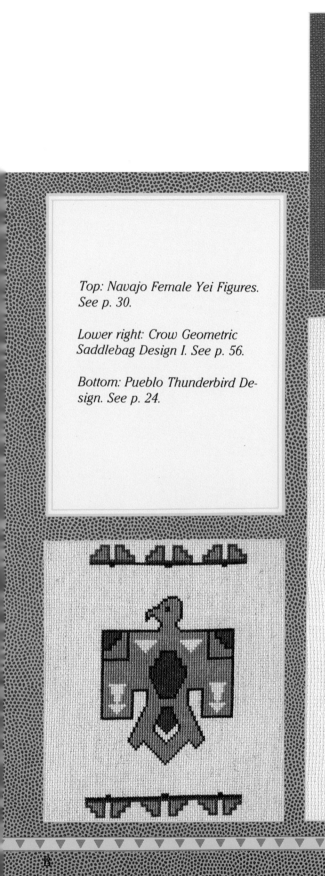

Left top: Pima Thunderbird Design. See p. 22.

Lower left: Plains Indian Geometric Design II. See p. 62.

Lower right: Blackfoot Tipi, Front View. See p. 48.

Top right: Hopi Adobe Dwelling. See p. 18.

Center right: Navajo Male Yei Figures. See p. 32.

Bottom right: Pacific Northwest Eagle. See p. 74.

Directly above: Navajo Rug Design I. See p. 26.

Top left: Sioux Mountains and Lakes (1-row version). See p. 52.

Bottom left: Zuni Raindancer. See p. 20.

Top right: Plains Indian Geometric Design I. See p. 60.

Bottom right: Pacific Northwest Raven with the Sun in His Beak. See p. 76.

Right: Plains Indian Saddlebag Design II. See p. 58.

Below: Blackfoot Three Tipis. (Also shown individually.) See p. 42.

Top left: Navajo Mother Earth and Father Sky. See p. 34.

Bottom left: Pacific Northwest Killer Whale Design. See p. 70.

Bottom right: Hopi Pottery Design. See p. 16.

Top: Pacific Northwest Totem Pole—Raven with Three Watchers. See p. 68.

Left top: Apache Thunderbird. See p. 36.

Left center: Iroquois Wampum Belt. See p. 85.

Bottom left: Navajo Rug Design II. See p. 28.

PACIFIC NORTHWEST DESIGNS

I like wood; I like to feel it.
Each different wood has its own purpose.
I make masks out of alder; it is light and hard.
We also use it for our bowls and spoons because it has no taste.
Yellow cedar has a strong taste when it gets wet.
Red cedar we use for our canoes and houses and large totem poles.
Birch is good for rattles; it is harder and gives a better sound.
—Dempsey Bob, Tahltan-Tlingit Artist

Reprinted with permission from *Indian Artists at Work*, by Ulli Steltzer, Seattle, Douglas & McIntyre/University of Washington Press, 1976.

PACIFIC NORTHWEST INDIANS

The highly skilled Pacific Northwest Indian artists are known internationally for their distinctive style of art, particularly their carving, weaving, and jewelry making. The special element of their art, a complex combination of curves, ovoids, inner ovoids and 'S' forms, is the filling in of these designs into a given form. The designs, of highly stylized animal and bird crests and totems, are fit onto sides of wooden boxes, onto dishes, silver jewelry, onto robes and other clothing; if the entire animal or bird design does not fit, it is rearranged with its body parts separated and placed at precise angles until all the parts fit into the pre-determined space.

The family and tribal crests of such animals and birds as the raven, bear, whale, salmon, and eagle, are a crucial part of the ceremony and daily lives of the Pacific Northwest Indians, and these crests are displayed on impressive cedar houseposts and totem poles, house fronts and screens, as well as on baskets, clothing, cedar boxes, canoes, ceremonial masks, and jewelry.

The colors used by the Northwest artist are soft tones of browns, lots of black, and touches of blue or turquoise and red or rust. The Haida used mostly red and black, although the designs in this volume include blues and gold. The colors, subjects, and mediums of the Northwest Indian artist reflect an outdoor life among forests of cedar, fir, hemlock and redwood, and a vital contact with the costal waters rich in sea life.

The tribes of the Northwest live from the panhandle of Alaska, through western Canada, Washington, Oregon, and a portion of northern California. Some of these tribes are the Haida, Kwakiutl, Tlingit, Salish, Chinook, Tsimshian, Klallam, Quileute, and Skagit.

TOTEM POLE—RAVEN WITH THREE WATCHERS HAIDA

FINISHED DESIGN ON 14-COUNT AIDA: 3″ × 8¾″.

Use ecru or off-white aida cloth or linen, or fiddler's cloth. For needlepoint, use an ivory or off-white yarn for the background.

Use DMC floss, 2 strands: Blue, 312; Brown, 975; Red, 817; Gold, 782. Use 2 skeins of Black and Gold, 1 skein of all other colors.

The Pacific Northwest totem poles are skillfully designed and carved wooden poles (usually of the native Northwest western red cedar) which reflect symbols, mythology, and historic facts of tribes or clans concerned. The Northwest carver was one of the most skilled carvers in America, carving entirely from memory to create the huge, impressive house posts and totem poles which exemplify Northwest Indian art.

The raising of a totem pole was a special event, and a potlatch celebration was given, with song, dance, food and gifts being presented.

The raven, depicted on the pole here, was a major part of the Northwest Indian mythology; Raven could do anything, know everything, and could change form at will, and in legend is credited with bringing sunlight to the world. Note the three watchers which sit atop the totem: the middle watcher keeps an eye out for the enemy outside the clan, and the watchers on either side are responsible for checking on the enemies from within the clan.

Many of these totems, with figures of bears, whales, beaver, eagles, and other clan and family crests can still be seen in Washington, Alaska, and Canada, although the oldest have given way to the elements of nature and are no longer in existence. The craft is still alive, and some excellent craftsmen are available to carve poles for ceremonial affairs, or for business and home decoration.

Illus. 48. Totem Pole—Raven with Three Watchers. In color on p. H of color section.

Illus. 49. Facing page: Totem Pole, Raven with Three Watchers Chart.

Symbol	Number	Color
o	310	Black
1	817	Red
–	975	Brown
.	312	Blue
All Unmarked Squares	782	Gold

KILLER WHALE DESIGN
TLINGIT

Illus. 50. Killer Whale Design. In color on p. G of color section.

FINISHED DESIGN ON 14-COUNT AIDA: 7″ × 6″.

Use ecru or off-white aida cloth or linen, or fiddler's cloth. For needlepoint, use ivory or off-white yarn for the background.

Use DMC floss, 2 skeins Black and Gold and 1 skein all other colors. Work in 2 strands. (This design may be worked in either of the color combinations; pictured is the rust/turquoise version.)

FOR RUST/TURQUOISE TONES (pictured in color section): Black, 310; Gold, 3045; Rust, 920; Turquoise, 991; Whale's teeth, 3046.
Or,

FOR RED/BLUE TONES (simply use red in place of the rust and the blue in place of the turquoise): Black, 310; Gold, 3045; Red, 817; Blue, 312; Whale's teeth, 3046.

The whale is a powerful spirit totem of the Pacific Northwest tribes. The family or clan represented by the whale are particularly skilled hunters of seals and water birds and are good fishermen of salmon and halibut. The whale is an often-used symbol commonly displayed in public places throughout the Northwest when Indian motifs are used and is noted by a long, large head, a dorsal fin, and a large mouth.

Illus. 51. Facing page: Killer Whale Design Chart.

Symbol	Number	Color
o	310	Black
1	817	Red
	OR	
	920	Rust
–	312	Blue
	OR	
	991	Turquoise
.	3045	Gold
*	3046	Light Gold (Whale Teeth)

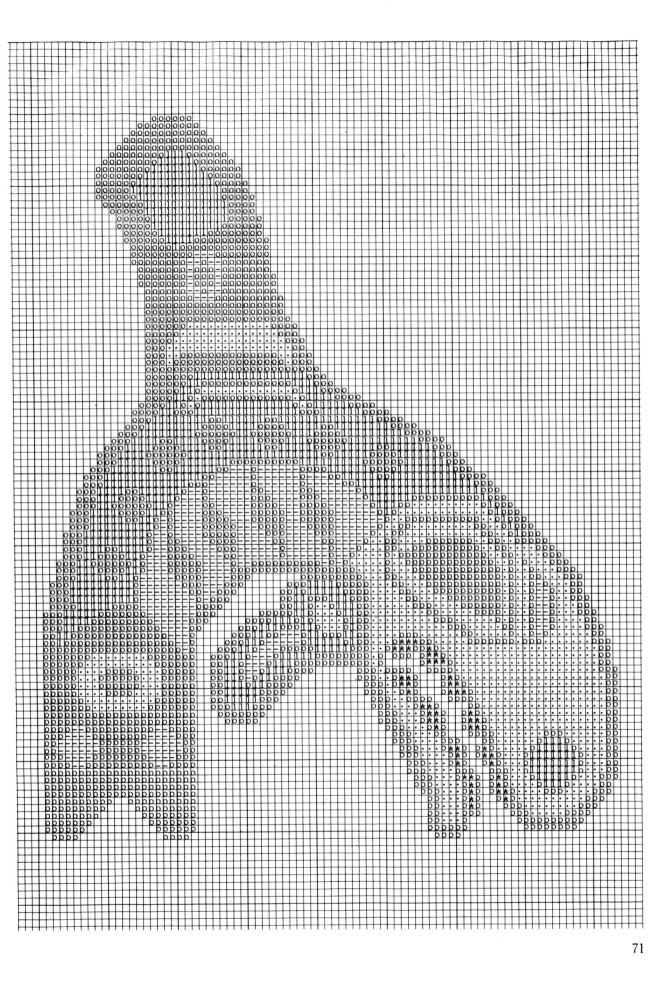

BEAR DESIGN
PACIFIC NORTHWEST

Illus. 52. Bear Design. In color on p. A of color section.

FINISHED DESIGN ON 14-COUNT AIDA: 7″ × 6″.

Use ecru or off-white aida cloth or linen, or fiddler's cloth. For needlepoint, use ivory or off-white yarn for the background.

Use DMC floss, 1 skein each color. Work in 2 strands. (The design may be worked in either of the color combinations listed below.)

FOR RUST/TURQUOISE TONES (pictured): Black, 310; Gold, 3045; Rust, 920; Turquoise, 991.
Or,

FOR RED/BLUE TONES (substitute the red in place of the rust, and the blue in place of the turquoise): Black, 310; Gold, 3045; Red, 817; Blue, 312.

The bear, either black or brown bear, is one of the most common spirit totems and guardian spirits of the Northwest Indian because of the animal's great strength. Bear is most usually shown with prominent teeth and a protruding tongue, as in this design, and is seen depicted in all areas of Pacific Northwest life on totem poles, clothing, jewelry, and cedar carvings. Please note that the background of the face, as it is worked here, takes artistic license, since black is usually the primary color in Northwest designs with the turquoise or red used only in smaller areas as a secondary color.

Illus. 53. Facing page: Bear Design Chart.

Symbol	Number	Color
X	3045	Gold
o	310	Black
–	920	Rust
	OR	
	817	Red
·	991	Turquoise
	OR	
	312	Blue

EAGLE DESIGN
HAIDA

Illus. 54. Eagle Design. In color on p. D of color section.

FINISHED DESIGN ON 14-COUNT AIDA: 4⅞″ × 11½″.

Use ecru or off-white aida or linen, or fiddler's cloth. For needlepoint, use ivory or off-white yarn for the background.

Use DMC floss, 2 skeins Black and Gold, 1 skein all other colors. Work in 2 strands.

(This design may be worked in either of the color combinations below; pictured is the red/blue design.)

FOR RED/BLUE TONES (pictured): Gold, 3045; Black, 310; Red, 817; Blue, 312; Ochre, 782.

Or,

FOR RUST/TURQUOISE TONES (simply substitute the rust for red, and turquoise for blue): Gold, 3045; Black, 310; Rust, 920; Turquoise, 991; Ochre, 782.

The eagle is considered to be one of the most powerful of the Pacific Northwest family and clan totem crests. The eagle can be seen displayed on silver jewelry, cedar boxes, woven blankets, totem poles, and other artistic items. The eagle endows qualities of good hunting and penetrating eyesight and is always portrayed with his beak curving downwards in designs. The eagle is often seen on totem poles with wings outstretched, as in this design.

This is a good-sized piece of work (not for beginners), and looks stunning either framed or as a pillow cover.

Illus. 55. Eagle Design Chart.

Symbol	Number	Color
o	310	Black
V	817	Red
	OR	
	920	Rust
+	312	Blue
	OR	
	991	Turquoise
–	782	Ochre
Unmarked Squares	3045	Gold

74

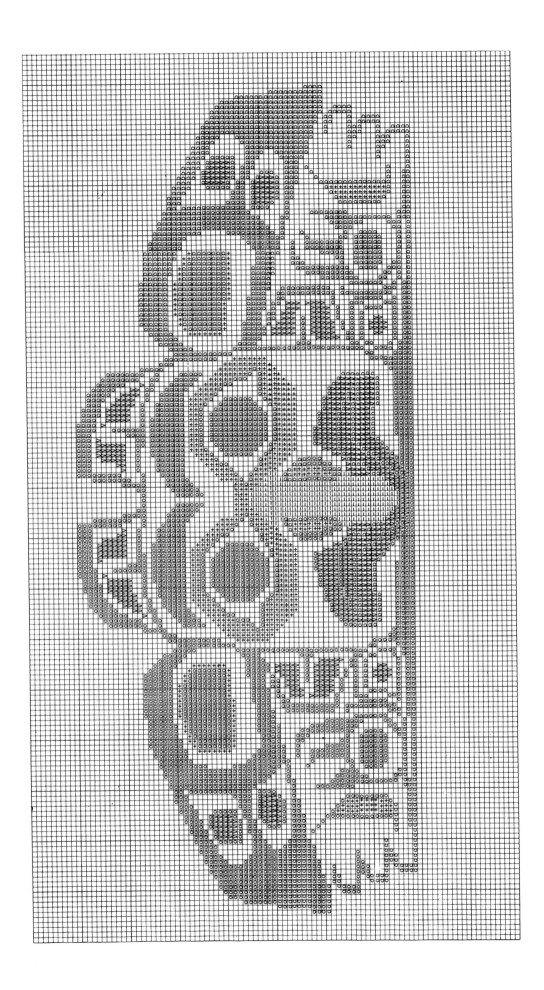

RAVEN WITH THE SUN IN HIS BEAK
HAIDA

Illus. 56. Raven with the Sun in his Beak. In color on
p. E of color section.

FINISHED DESIGN ON 14-COUNT AIDA: 8″ × 9″.

Use ecru or off-white aida cloth or linen, or fiddler's cloth. For needlepoint, use ivory or off-white yarn for the background.

Use DMC floss, 2 strands: Black, 310; Gold, 3045; Rust, 920; Turquoise, 991; and the sun in Raven's beak should be Red, 817. Use 2 skeins Black and Gold, and 1 skein of the other colors.

The raven is shown here as he is often depicted, with a sun disc in his partially open beak, to show that Raven, according to legend, tossed the sun into the sky to bring light to the world. Raven is distinguished by a long, straight beak with a blunt, turned-down tip, and usually a tongue. Raven is very powerful, and can turn himself into any other animal, human, or inanimate form and is the subject of many Northwest legends and stories.

Illus. 57. Facing page: Raven with the Sun in His Beak Chart.

Symbol	Number	Color
o	310	Black
.	3045	Gold
–	817	Red
	OR	
	920	Rust
1	312	Blue
	OR	
	991	Turquoise
X	817	Red (The Sun)

76

EASTERN WOODLAND AND NORTH-EASTERN DESIGNS

←――――――――――――→

MY BARK CANOE

In the still night, the long night through,
I guide my bark canoe,
My love, to you.
While the stars shine, and falls the dew,
I seek my love in bark canoe—
I seek for you.
It is I, love, your lover true,
Who glides the stream in bark canoe.
It glides to you.
My love, to you.
—Ojibway

From *American Indian Love Lyrics*, selected by Nellie Barnes. Copyright 1925. Reprinted with permission of Macmillan Publishing Company, New York.

EASTERN WOODLAND AND NORTHEASTERN INDIANS

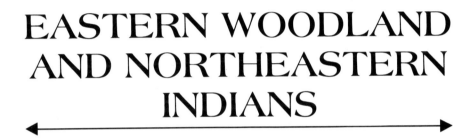

The art of the Eastern Woodland tribes was notably the quill and later the beadwork. Geometric designs were popular, and later European-influenced floral designs took hold and were used to decorate all types of clothing and accessories. Basket-weaving was very popular and the styles and techniques were impressive; the baskets were used for making carrying baskets, fish traps, and sieves. Fishing and farming was the way of life in this region, which essentially was the area from the edge of the Plains eastward through the Great Lakes area. The Eastern Woodland tribes lived in wigwams, which were round huts covered with birchbark and rush mats.

The Northeastern tribes also did excellent work in quills and beads, and also made pottery as well as baskets. The Iroquois are known for their wampum belts (see wampum belt design). The Iroquois, who are also noted for their advanced system of government, formed the Five Nations Confederation, which included the element of elected representatives, and it is said that the Iroquois system was studied by the founders of the United States Constitution.

There were many other tribes in the eastern part of the country, from New York and Pennsylvania to Florida, westward to Minnesota and Wisconsin. Several tribes (such as the Cherokee, Chickasaw, and Choctaw) were forced from their homes in the East to the plains of Oklahoma, Arkansas and Kansas. Other Eastern tribes were the Shawnee, Cree, Delaware and Ojibway.

HEADBAND DESIGN
OJIBWAY

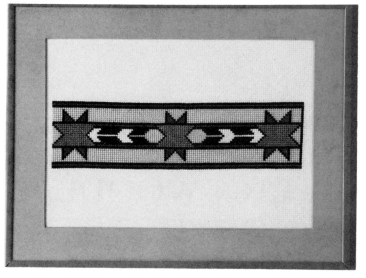

Illus. 58. Ojibway Headband. In color on p. A of color section.

FINISHED DESIGN ON 14 COUNT AIDA: 2¼″ × 9″.

Use white, beige, or unbleached aida cloth or linen. It is best to use a large piece (8″ × 14″ approx.) to give room for embroidery hoop, and cut to fit later, if making a headband.

Use DMC floss, 2 strands: Red, 666; Grey, 414; Yellow, 726; White; Black. You will need 1 skein of each color.

The Objibwa lived in the area of the Great Lakes. They are known for their brightly colored quill and beadwork; they used both geometrical designs (shown here), and elaborate floral designs on their clothing, bags, and other accessories.

This is a brightly colored piece, which works well as hatband, headband, and clothing insert. It can be deceiving, since it actually looks beaded when used as a hatband. To make a hatband, measure the length needed, and repeat design lengthwise to desired length. Sew ends together and hand-hem, slipping it over the hat.

To make a headband, measure length needed, repeat design lengthwise to desired length. Hem by hand on all sides. Attach ties to four corners and tie, or stitch band together at ends for slip-over headband.

To make a very striking pillow design, stitch 3 rows of the design with long sides touching. Do *not* repeat the black-red-black border; rather, only stitch the black-red-black border once each time, with yellow on each side of the border. Pillow design measures approximately 7″ × 9″.

Illus. 59. Facing page: Ojibway Headband Design Chart.

Symbol	Number	Color
1	666	Red
z	444	Grey
–		White
.	726	Yellow
o	310	Black

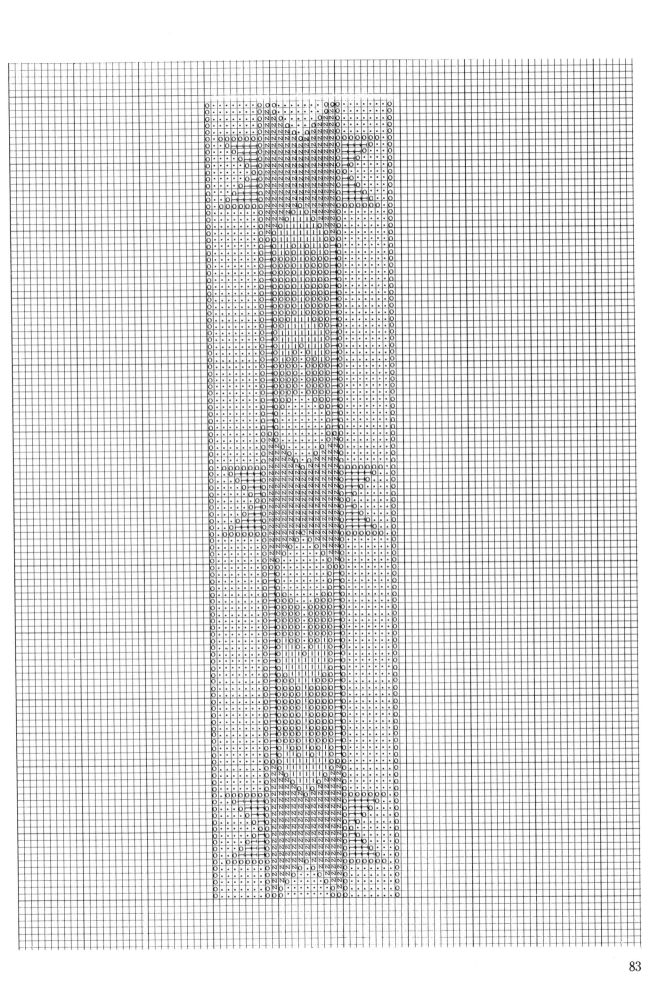

Illus. 60. Three-Row Ojibway Design Chart (Color Code on p. 82).

WAMPUM BELT DESIGN
IROQUOIS

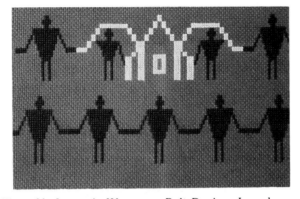

Illus. 61. Iroquois Wampum Belt Design. In color on p. H of color section.

FINISHED DESIGN ON 14-COUNT AIDA: 8″ × 10″.

Use rust-colored aida cloth or linen. For needlepoint, use rust-colored yarn for the background.

Use DMC floss, 3 strands: Bright Blue, 820; Purple, 550; Cream, 712. Use 1 skein of each color.

(If a light color of fabric is substituted for the rust, you will need to substitute Black floss, 310, for the Cream, 712.)

This design was adapted from the famous Iroquois wampum belts. The Iroquois are noted for these unusual belts, which were used for agreements and treaties and usually indicated an end to a particular conflict. The belts were made of what is called wampum, which were small tubular beads of white and deep purple shells; the belts were woven into a strip, and the design extended the length of the belt. (The word "wampum" comes from an Algonquian word, "wampumpeag," which meant cylindrical shell beads.)

The design shown here has been adapted to use in the making of a pillow or for framing. It may also be used for borders or belts by simply extending the design of the figures as long as is needed for the border or belt. (The center pattern, with the cream-colored house structure, would be the center of the border or belt, and the figures would alternate in color, extending from either side of the center figures, as long as is needed for decorative purposes.)

Illus. 62. Iroquois Wampum Belt Chart on following page.

Symbol	Number	Color
s	712	Cream
x	550	Purple
o	820	Blue

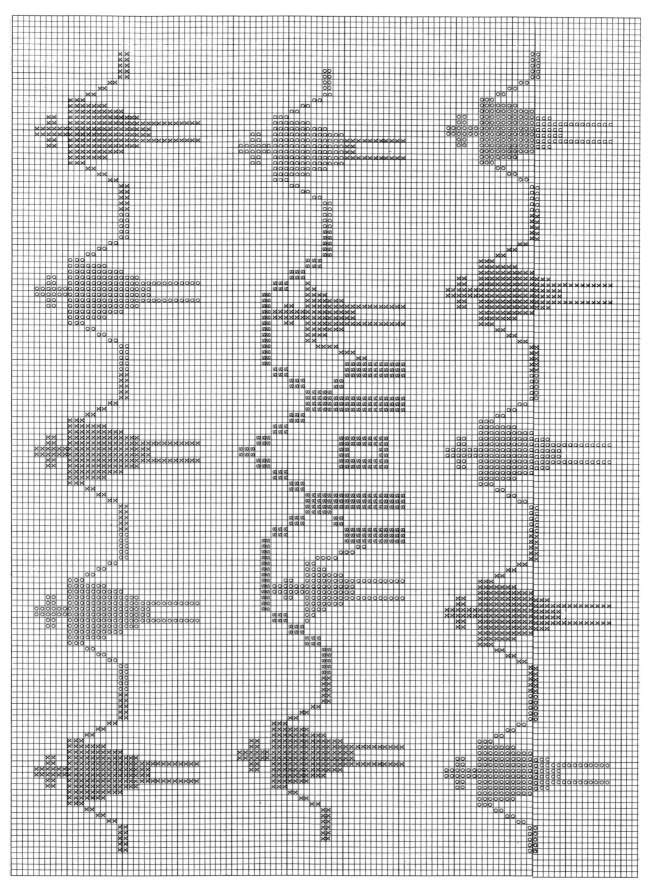

86

ALPHABET
CHEROKEE

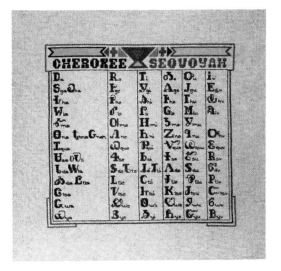

Illus. 63. Cherokee Alphabet as Created by Sequoyah.
In color on back cover.

FINISHED DESIGN SIZE ON 18-COUNT FABRIC: 10¾″ × 10¼″.

Model is stitched on 18-count Floba, a fabric of linen and rayon. Fiddler's cloth, 18- or 14-count, is also recommended.

Use DMC floss: Green, 701; Yellow, 444; Red, 666; Bright Blue, 995; Fuschia, 718; Orange, 971; Dark Blue, 820; Rust, 919; Dark Red, 304; Purple, 550; Turquoise/Green, 991; and Rust/Orange, 900.

For backstitching, use the following: Match small backstitched letters with the larger cross-stitched letters in the same column, i.e.: 1st column of backstitched letters should be blue to match the 820 blue. 2nd column of backstitched letters should be rust to match the 919 rust. 3rd column of backstitched letters should be dark red, to match the 304 red. 4th column of backstitched letters should be purple, to match the 550 purple. 5th column of backstitched letters should be turquoise to match the 991 turquoise. 6th column of backstitched letters should be rust/orange to match the 900 orange.

Backstitched lines to separate the columns should be stitched as follows: Lines to the LEFT, ABOVE, and BELOW each column of letters should MATCH the letters in that column, for ex-ample: the lines to the LEFT, ABOVE, and BELOW the 1st column of blue 820 letters should be 820 blue, to match.

The last line on the right of the last column of orange 900 should be stitched in 900 orange also, so that the last column will have matching back-stitched lines to the RIGHT, as well as to the LEFT, ABOVE, and BELOW.

This Cherokee alphabet was created by Se-quoyah, over a period of several years in the early 1800's. The alphabet enabled the Cherokee people to read, publish newspapers and books, and to establish their own schools.

The Cherokee people lived in the southern Appalachian mountains, but in the late 1830's, were forced from their lands by the U.S. government, and were moved on foot to what was then Indian Territory, now Oklahoma. Many of the Cherokee perished along the way, and the journey is known as the Trail of Tears. A few of the Cherokee hid and stayed in the South, so that now there are Cherokee settlements both in the South and in Oklahoma.

The Cherokee art combines bright colors and geometric forms, and, occasionally, included Eu-ropean-influenced floral designs.

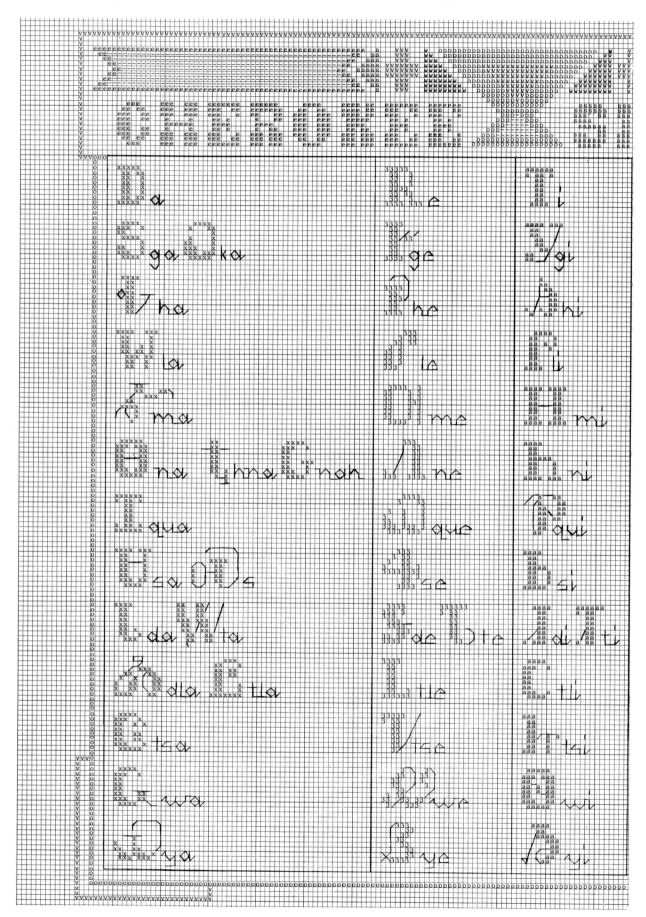

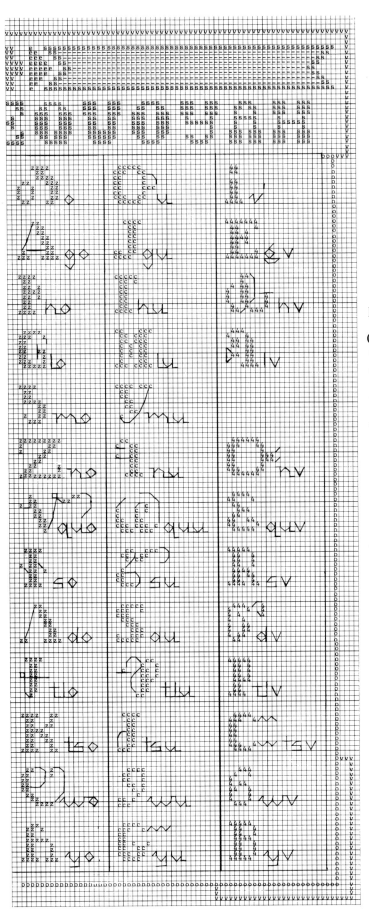

Illus. 64. Cherokee Alphabet Chart.

COLOR CHART FOR CHEROKEE ALPHABET

←—————————————————→

o	701	Green (in upper border)
—	444	Yellow (in upper border)
e	666	Red (letters of 'cherokee' and small triangle in upper border)
s	995	Bright Blue (letters of 'sequoyah' and small triangle in upper border)
v	718	Fuchsia (top border and small borders at bottom corners of chart)
w	971	Orange (in upper border)

Alphabet letters

x	820	Blue	first column
3	919	Brown	second column
a	304	Dark Red	third column
z	550	Purple	fourth column
c	991	Turquoise/Green	fifth column
4	900	Rust/Orange	last column

See above instructions for the backstitching colors.

APPENDICES

BIBLIOGRAPHY

The following books are recommended for those interested in studying further the Indian crafts that influenced the designs shown here. Most can be found in any reference library.

Appleton, LeRoy H. *Indian Art of the Americas*, New York: Charles Scribner's Sons, 1950.

Bancroft-Hunt, Norman and Werner Forman. *The Indians of the Great Plains*. London: Orbis Publishing, Ltd., 1981.

Covarrubias, M. *The Eagle, the Jaguar, and the Serpent*. New York: Alfred Knopf, 1954.

Davis, Christopher. *North American Indian*. London: The Hamlyn Publishing Group, Ltd., 1969.

Erdoes, Richard. *The Rain Dance People*. New York: Alfred Knopf, 1976.

Fox, Frank. *North American Indians*. Los Angeles: Troubador Press, 1986.

Glubok, Shirley. *The Art of the North American Indian*. New York: Harper & Row, 1964.

Harmsen, W.D., ed. *Patterns and Sources of Navajo Weaving*. Harmsen's Western Americana Collection, 1977.

Houston, James, Ed. and Illustrator. *Songs of the Dream People*. New York: Atheneum, 1972.

Hungry Wolf, Adolf. *Tipi Life*. Alberta, Sask.: Good Medicine Books, 1972.

Hunt, W. Ben and J. F. "Buck" Burshears. *American Indian Beadwork*. New York: Macmillan Publishing Co., 1951.

Indian Arts & Crafts Board and U.S. Department of Interior. *Painted Tipis by Contemporary Plains Indian Artists*, 1973.

Marriott, Alice. *Indians of the Four Corners*. New York: T.Y. Crowell Press, Inc., 1952.

Mason, Bernard S. *The Book of Indian Crafts and Costumes*. New York: A. S. Barnes & Co., 1946.

McConkey, Lois, illustrated by Douglas Tait. *Sea and Cedar*. Madrona Press, 1973.

McLuhan, T. C. *Touch the Earth*. New York: Outerbridge and Dienstfrey, 1973.

Sheppard, Sally. *Indians of the Eastern Woodlands*. New York: Franklin Watts, Inc., 1975.

Steltzer, Ulli. *Indian Artist at Work*. Seattle and London: University of Washington Press, 1976.

Whiteford, Andrew Hunter. *North American Indian Arts*. New York: Golden Press, 1970.

METRIC EQUIVALENCY CHART

MM—MILLIMETRES   CM—CENTIMETRES

INCHES TO MILLIMETRES AND CENTIMETRES

INCHES	MM	CM	INCHES	CM	INCHES	CM
⅛	3	0.3	9	22.9	30	76.2
¼	6	0.6	10	25.4	31	78.7
⅜	10	1.0	11	27.9	32	81.3
½	13	1.3	12	30.5	33	83.8
⅝	16	1.6	13	33.0	34	86.4
¾	19	1.9	14	35.6	35	88.9
⅞	22	2.2	15	38.1	36	91.4
1	25	2.5	16	40.6	37	94.0
1¼	32	3.2	17	43.2	38	96.5
1½	38	3.8	18	45.7	39	99.1
1¾	44	4.4	19	48.3	40	101.6
2	51	5.1	20	50.8	41	104.1
2½	64	6.4	21	53.3	42	106.7
3	76	7.6	22	55.9	43	109.2
3½	89	8.9	23	58.4	44	111.8
4	102	10.2	24	61.0	45	114.3
4½	114	11.4	25	63.5	46	116.8
5	127	12.7	26	66.0	47	119.4
6	152	15.2	27	68.6	48	121.9
7	178	17.8	28	71.1	49	124.5
8	203	20.3	29	73.7	50	127.0

YARDS TO METRES

YARDS	METRES	YARDS	METRES	YARDS	METRES	YARDS	METRES	YARDS	METRES
⅛	0.11	2⅛	1.94	4⅛	3.77	6⅛	5.60	8⅛	7.43
¼	0.23	2¼	2.06	4¼	3.89	6¼	5.72	8¼	7.54
⅜	0.34	2⅜	2.17	4⅜	4.00	6⅜	5.83	8⅜	7.66
½	0.46	2½	2.29	4½	4.11	6½	5.94	8½	7.77
⅝	0.57	2⅝	2.40	4⅝	4.23	6⅝	6.06	8⅝	7.89
¾	0.69	2¾	2.51	4¾	4.34	6¾	6.17	8¾	8.00
⅞	0.80	2⅞	2.63	4⅞	4.46	6⅞	6.29	8⅞	8.12
1	0.91	3	2.74	5	4.57	7	6.40	9	8.23
1⅛	1.03	3⅛	2.86	5⅛	4.69	7⅛	6.52	9⅛	8.34
1¼	1.14	3¼	2.97	5¼	4.80	7¼	6.63	9¼	8.46
1⅜	1.26	3⅜	3.09	5⅜	4.91	7⅜	6.74	9⅜	8.57
1½	1.37	3½	3.20	5½	5.03	7½	6.86	9½	8.69
1⅝	1.49	3⅝	3.31	5⅝	5.14	7⅝	6.97	9⅝	8.80
1¾	1.60	3¾	3.43	5¾	5.26	7¾	7.09	9¾	8.92
1⅞	1.71	3⅞	3.54	5⅞	5.37	7⅞	7.20	9⅞	9.03
2	1.83	4	3.66	6	5.49	8	7.32	10	9.14

EMBROIDERY THREAD CONVERSION CHART

⟵⟶

DMC	COATS & CLARK	BATES/ANCHOR	DMC	COATS & CLARK	BATES/ANCHOR
300	352	•	780	•	310
304	47	3401	782	•	308
310	403	8403	783	•	307
311	149	7980	793	•	121
312	147	7979	796	7100	133
316	895	3081	798	7022	131
317	400	8512	801	5475	357
321	47	3500	807	7168	168
322	978	7978	809	7021	130
326	59	3401	815	3000	43
336	149	7981	817	2335	19
356	5975	2338	820	7024	134
			839	5360	380
414	400	8513	840	5379	379
420	375	5374	898	5476	360
422	373	5372	900	2329	333
434	309	5000	912	6205	205
444	291	2298	919	2326	341
445	288	2288	920	3337	339
			922	3336	324
517	169	7162	938	5477	381
518	168	•	950	2336	4146
550	102	4107	955	6030	206
552	101	4092	958	6186	187
553	98	4097	959	6186	186
			971	2099	316
601	78	3128	973	2290	290
666	46	3046	975	5349	355
699	923	6228	989	6266	242
			991	6212	189
701	227	6226	993	6185	186
702	239	6239	995	7010	410
712	387	5387	3045	2412	373
718	88	•	3046	2410	887
721	324	•	3051	6317	846
725	306	2298	3064	•	914
726	295	2294	3371	5478	382
729	890	•	3687	3088	69
738	942	5375	3688	3087	66
740	316	2099	3689	3086	49
743	297	2302			

INDEX